101 OFFENSIVE BASKETBALL DRILLS

George Karl
Terry Stotts
Price Johnson

ISBN: 1-57167-078-5

Book Layout: Michelle A. Summers
Diagrams: Julie L. Denzer and Michelle A. Summers
Developmental Editor: Joanna Wright
Cover Design: Deborah M. Bellaire and Julie L. Denzer
Cover Photos: Courtesy of the NBA
                 Andy Hayt

Coaches Choice Books is an imprint of: Sagamore Publishing, Inc.
                                           P.O. Box 647
                                           Champaign, IL 61824-0647
                                           (217) 359-5940
                                           Fax: (217) 359-5975
                                           Web Site: http//www.sagamorepub.com

CONTENTS

Chapter

ACKNOWLEDGMENTS

The authors would like to thank John Sullivan for his editorial assistance in helping to write up drills presented in this book. The authors are also grateful for the professional assistance in publishing this book provided by the staff of Coaches Choice Books and Videos—particularly Michelle Summers, Joanna Wright, Debbie Bellaire and Julie Denzer.

Finally, special thanks are extended to all of the players and coaches with whom we have had the opportunity to work with over the years. Their efforts and feedback have helped influence the design and ultimately the selection of the drills included in this book.

DEDICATION

This book is dedicated to our families—who motivated us to strive for excellence and reach for new heights. Their love enriches and energizes us.

George Karl
Terry Stotts
Price Johnson

PREFACE

For the more than three decades that I have been playing and coaching basketball, I have observed countless situations on the court and literally thousands of individuals attempting to play the game to the best of their abilities. Collectively, my experiences have given me an opportunity to evaluate many techniques and fundamentals for playing competitive basketball and a variety of methods for teaching those techniques and fundamentals. In the process, I have come to realize that true learning occurs when there is a need to know, a solid understanding of how to learn exists, and coaches and players realize that a particular goal can be reached.

My co-authors and I wrote this book to provide basketball coaches at all competitive levels with a tool that can enable them to maximize the skills and attributes of their players. As a vehicle for teaching and learning, properly designed drills can have extraordinary value. Each of the four volumes of drills in this series features drills that I have collected, court-tested, and applied over the course of my coaching career. If in the process of using the drills presented in this book coaches are better able to develop the skills of their players, then the effort to write these drill books will have been well worthwhile.

George Karl

DIAGRAM KEY

G	— guard
PG	— point guard
SG	— shooting guard
F	— forward
SF	— small forward
PF	— power forward
C	— center

—————————————➤ —movement of a player

∿∿∿∿∿∿∿∿∿➤ —movement of a player dribbling the basketball

——————————⊥ —movement of a player executing a screen

— — — — — — ➤ —movement of the basketball via a pass

CHAPTER 1

CONDITIONING DRILLS

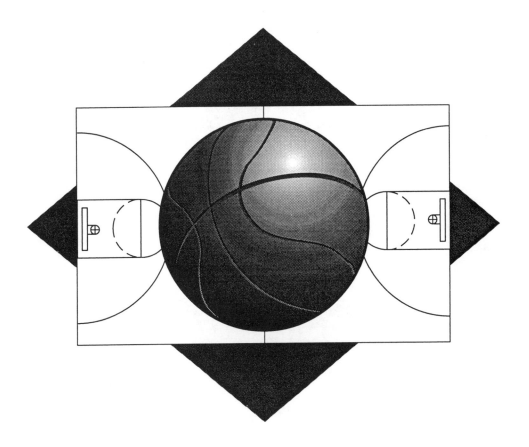

Drill #1: Shuffle On Command

Objective: To warm up; to improve the ability to move laterally; to enhance conditioning level.

Description: The players spread out facing the coach, at least double-arms length from their nearest teammate. Using a basketball as a directional pointer, the coach signals the players to perform a series of specific movements; for example, power shuffle to the left or right, back shuffle (defensive slide), back pedal, run in place, etc. The players respond to the coach's signals.

Coaching Point:

- As the drill progresses and the players begin to get warmed up, the time between each directional signal by the coach should be shortened.

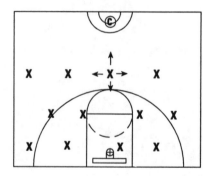

Drill #2: Four Corner Warm-Up Drill

Objective: To warm up; to practice passing skills, footwork, lay-up shooting, and rebounding techniques.

Description: The drill begins with five players positioned as shown in Diagram 2. X3 begins the drill with a cross court pass to X4. On the pass, X1 (the shooter) and X2 (the rebounder/outlet passer) break to the basket. X4 then passes in the corner to X5, who hits X1 in full stride for a lay-up. X1 goes up for the shot off the pass, never putting the ball on the floor. X2 rebounds the ball and passes it to X3. Players rotate counter-clockwise with the drill continuing on a non-stop basis. The ball movement can reversed in order to give the players the opportunity to work on shooting lay-ups with their opposite hand. When using the drill in a practice situation, the coach can add an element of conditioning by placing penalties for errant passes, the ball hitting the floor, or missed lay-ups (e.g., sprints, sit-ups, or push-ups).

Coaching Points:

- Emphasis should be placed on the ball never hitting the floor.
- The player shooting a lay-up should be encouraged to keep the ball above shoulder level.
- The drill should begin with one ball and build up to two or three balls as the players' level of proficiency develops.

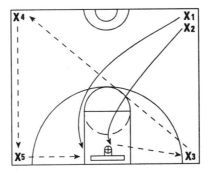

Drill #3: 4-Minute Drill

Objective: To develop stamina; to practice shooting lay-ups and jump-shots.

Description: This drill involves five players at a time. Players X1, X2, and X3 begin the drill by performing a three-person straight line fast break to the other basket. The ball is passed back and forth between the players and is not allowed to touch the floor. Once the ball arrives at the other basket, X3 shoots a lay-up. X1 and X2 stop at the elbow of the lane. After receiving passes from X4 and X5 who are positioned outside the baseline, X1 and X2 shoot a jump-shot. X3 rebounds his own shot and takes the middle as X3, X4, and X5 straight line fast break in the other direction. The basic goal is to try to make 100 baskets (total of lay-ups and jump-shots) in four minutes.

Coaching Point:

- Maintaining the proper position on the break should be emphasized.

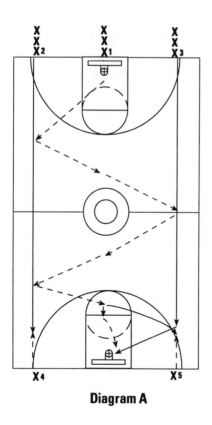

Diagram A

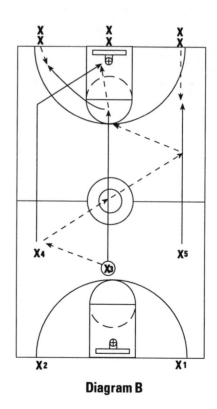

Diagram B

Drill #4: Box Race

Objective: To develop stamina; to practice dribbling with both hands.

Description: The coach positions four cones in a box-like alignment on one end of the court. Four players, each with a basketball, participate in the drill at a time—one starting at each of the four cones. On a command from the coach, the players dribble clockwise around the outside of the cones using a left-hand dribble. Each player tries to catch the player ahead. After a predetermined number of trips around the cones, the coach has the players change direction and move counter-clockwise around the cones using a right-hand dribble.

Coaching Point:

- The importance of being able to control the ball and adhere to proper dribbling fundamentals while moving quickly should be emphasized.

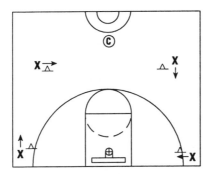

Drill #5: Loose Ball Scramble Drill

Objective: To enhance conditioning while hustling for a loose ball; to practice picking up a loose ball; to improve the footwork skills involved in pivoting to the basket.

Description: The entire team is involved in this drill. The coach assumes a position under the basket with the ball. Two lines of players are positioned equal distance from the center of the free throw line. With the players paired up by size, the coach begins the drill by rolling the ball toward the center of the free throw line. When the ball touches the foul line, the first player in each line breaks for the loose ball. The first player to the ball picks it up and executes a pivot and drives to the basket. The other player reacts and plays aggressive defense. The coach can require the pair to play a one-on-one game until one of them scores.

Coaching Point:

- The coach should emphasize proper footwork on the pivot and encourage an aggressive move to the hoop.

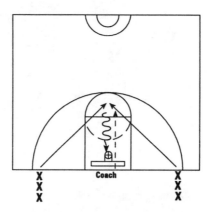

CHAPTER 2

BALL-HANDLING DRILLS

Drill #6: Forward-Backward Dribble Drill

Objective: To improve dribbling skills under simulated game conditions.

Description: This drill is appropriate for the entire team. Players should be grouped in pairs. One player has a ball and stands straddling a line on the court (e.g., baseline, sideline, half-court line) and facing the other player, who acts as a monitor. The player with the ball dribbles forward, pushing the ball out and backward, pulling the ball back. The second player makes sure the dribbler is going somewhere with every dribble. He should hold up a hand with an arbitrary number of fingers raised and have the dribbler call out the number of fingers to make him keep his head up while dribbling. After 30 seconds the players should switch roles. The drill should then be repeated using the opposite hand. The coach may choose to add a third player to each group as a defender. This variation helps develop floor vision by forcing the dribbler to look beyond the defender in order to call out the numbers correctly.

Coaching Point:

- The emphasis should be on dribbling with the proper push and pull techniques and keeping the head up while dribbling.

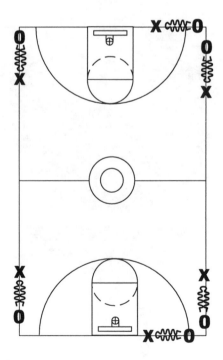

Drill #7: Pull-Back Crossover Drill

Objective: To practice the pull-back crossover dribble; to enhance conditioning levels.

Description: This drill begins with one player holding a ball and straddling a line on the court. Another player assumes a good defensive position. The first player takes two hard dribbles forward on one side of the line, then executes a pull-back, crossover maneuver across the line. The dribbler should be going backward with the crossover move faster than the defender is going forward. The dribbler swings his trail leg with the ball, making sure the crossover dribble is behind the original body position. After two minutes, the players switch roles. The coach may wish to add a third player behind the defender to hold up an arbitrary number of fingers, forcing the dribbler to call out the number of fingers.

Coaching Point:

- The coach should emphasize keeping the head up and moving forward with the dribble.

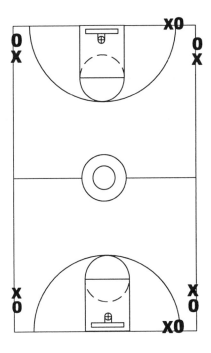

Drill #8: Down the Line Drill

Objective: To develop all aspects of ball-handling skills.

Description: Each player takes two dribbles down one side of a line on the court. On the third dribble, he pushes the ball over the line, but pulls it back before it hits the floor. This action is designed to practice ball control and ball movement as the player continues down the line. As the player progresses down the line, a head and shoulder fake and change of pace moves are added to the routine.

Coaching Point:

- The primary emphasis should be placed on good ball-handling and on keeping the player's head up while dribbling.

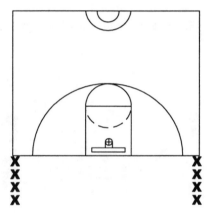

Drill #9: Pull-Back Spin Dribble Drill

Objective: To improve dribbling skills under simulated game conditions.

Description: The players should be grouped in pairs. One player has a ball and straddles a line on the court, while his teammate takes a defensive position. The first player dribbles forward and executes a spin move on the dribble. He plants his lead foot and pivots, while simultaneously pulling the ball back away from the defender. The dribbler accelerates out of the spin, staying as close to the original line as possible. The drill continues for two minutes, and then the players switch roles. The coach may have the dribbler execute a half-spin instead of the full spin and keep going in the same direction. He may also choose to add a third player positioned behind the defender. Similar to previous drills, this player can hold up an arbitrary number of fingers and require the dribbler to call out the number of fingers.

Coaching Point:

- The coach should make sure the dribbler comes out of the spin faster than he went into it and that the dribbler keeps his head up.

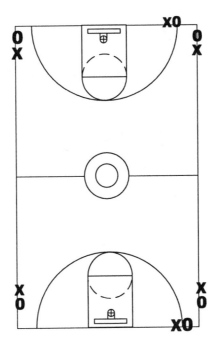

Drill #10: Scramble Tag

Objective: To improve dribbling skills in a fast-paced competitive atmosphere; to enhance stamina; to have fun.

Description: This drill is confined to the half-court. Each player has a ball and must dribble throughout the entire drill. Two players are singled out to be "it." These players must hold one hand in the air until they tag another player. The rest of the players try to evade the players who are "it." The players who are not "it" must dribble continuously and stay in bounds. Players who lose control of the ball or go out of bounds become "it." Players who lose control of the ball while attempting to tag another player retain their "it" designation.

Coaching Points:

- The coach may vary the duration of the drill according to the conditioning level of the team.
- The coach may wish to have all players dribble with their off hand.

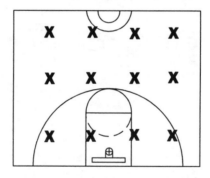

Drill #11: Two Ball Tag-Team Drill

Objective: To improve players' ability to dribble at full speed with either hand.

Description: The team is split into two equal groups, with half of each group positioned behind each baseline. On the whistle, the first player from each team dribbles two basketballs, one with each hand, to the opposite baseline as quickly as possible. There he tags his teammate, who takes the balls and dribbles in the other direction. If a player loses control of a ball, he must return to his starting point and begin again. The first team to have all its players complete the drill wins. The coach may use only one ball per team and specify whether the players are to use their strong or weak hand.

Coaching Point:

- The coach should stress to players the importance of keeping their heads up while dribbling.

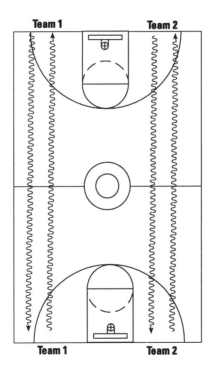

Drill #12: King of the Hill

Objective: To improve players' ability to protect the ball in a competitive situation.

Description: This drill begins with five players positioned inside the circle at the free throw lane. On a signal from the coach, players begin dribbling. Each player attempts to knock the other players' ball out of the circle while protecting his own dribble. When a player's ball is knocked out, that player is eliminated. Play continues until only one player remains in the circle. The coach may wish to have each player who is eliminated run full court sprints to add competition and inject a conditioning element into the drill.

Coaching Point:

- The emphasis should be on having players keep their heads up while dribbling and being aware of where other players are located.

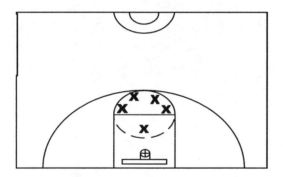

Drill #13: Keep-Away Dribble Drill

Objective: To develop the player's ability to control the ball while dribbling under defensive pressure.

Description: This drill is conducted at full speed. It begins at the midcourt line with one player on offense and the other assuming a defensive position. On the whistle, the offensive player begins dribbling the ball with the goal of controlling the ball on the dribble as long as possible. The defender does all he can to steal the ball or force his opponent to lose control or pick up his dribble. Players switch roles when the dribbler loses control of the ball or picks up his dribble. The coach can increase the difficulty of the drill by adding a second defensive player, thereby creating a two-on-one situation. The level of difficulty of the drill can also be increased by limiting the area in which the offensive player can work (i.e., half of a half-court).

Coaching Point:

- The coach should stress the use of both hands, crossover dribbles, and spin moves, all executed with the head up.

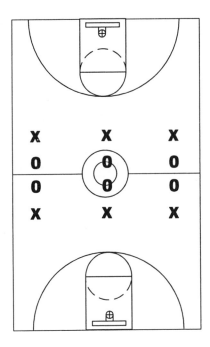

Drill #14: Basketball Scramble

Objective: To practice dribbling skills in a competitive atmosphere; to enhance conditioning level.

Description: The drill begins with five players on the baseline and four basketballs positioned on the free throw line. On a signal from the coach, the players scramble to gain possession of a ball. The four successful players dribble in the front court, while the fifth player attempts to steal a ball. When the designated time period (30 seconds to a minute) is up, the player without a ball is eliminated and must run line sprints. The drill is continued with four players and three balls and so on, until only two players and one ball remain.

Coaching Points:

- The coach may vary the length of the time period according the amount of conditioning desired.
- Decreasing the size of the area in which the four successful scramblers may dribble increases the emphasis on protecting the ball on the dribble.

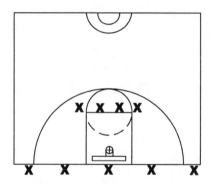

Drill #15: Zig-Zag Dribble Drill

Objective: To increase players' ability to bring a ball upcourt while under intense one-on-one pressure.

Description: The drill begins with two players, each with a ball, at one end of the court. The other two players are told to play aggressive defense. The offensive players begin their dribble to one side. After two dribbles, the defense attacks, aggressively attempting to steal the ball, cut off the line of the dribble, and body-check the dribbler. The offensive players are restricted to operating on one half of the court. When the dribblers get past the defense, they drive for a short pull-up jumper in the lane. Players then reverse their roles, and the drill continues in the other direction. With players of lesser skill levels, the coach may decrease the level of defensive pressure and designate points on the floor where the players should change directions.

Coaching Point:

- The emphasis should be placed on protecting the ball and moving upcourt using crossover, full-spin, and half-spin techniques.

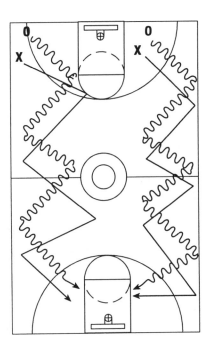

Drill #16: Jab-Crossover Drive Drill

Objective: To develop the footwork and dribbling skills necessary to execute a jab-crossover dribble drive.

Description: The coach separates the team into two lines, one on offense, the other on defense. Players rotate from one line to the other. The offensive player begins the drill by taking a jab step to his right. The defense shuts off the move, forcing the offensive player to execute the crossover move. The player pivots on the left foot, the right leg crosses over, and the dribble is shifted to the left hand. The dribbler's body should remain between the defender and the ball. After executing the crossover dribble, the player drives toward the basket. The same drill can be run from the opposite side of the court with the footwork and dribbling skills reversed. The drill may be run from the top of the key or from either wing.

Coaching Point:

- The emphasis should be placed on the sharpness of the cut and the quickness of the crossover move.

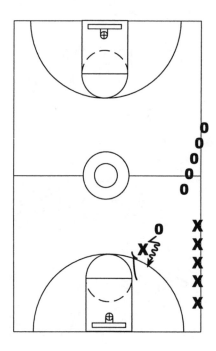

CHAPTER 3

SCREENING DRILLS

Drill #17: Fake and Replace

Objective: To practice setting a fake screen away; to develop offensive moves.

Description: This drill involves three players at a time—a guard and two wings. The drill begins with X1 executing a jab step at an imaginary opponent and coming back toward X3. X3 the passes the ball to X1, goes away from the pass to set a screen for X2, and then comes back to replace himself. X2 initially fakes coming to the top of the key and then cuts to the basket. X1 either shoots a jump-shot or passes the ball to X2, who shoots a lay-up.

Coaching Point:

- Offensive players should learn how to properly fake setting a screen.

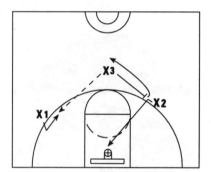

Drill #18: Three Player Screen Away Drill

Objective: To develop the footwork, passing, and screening skills necessary to execute the pass and screen away play.

Description: The coach should divide the team into groups of three. The drill begins with one group positioned as shown in Diagram 18. X1 passes the ball to the wing, X2, who has executed the jab-crossover without the ball in an effort to get open for the pass. X1 then moves to set a screen for X3, who cuts sharply off the screen to the basket, looking for the pass from X2. X1 then pops out looking for the pass to take the jump-shot. X2 passes the ball to the open player. As players' skills improve, the coach may want to add one or more defenders to add difficulty to the drill.

Coaching Points:

- The emphasis should be on using proper footwork when working without the ball and coming off a screen.
- The coach should stress maintaining proper spacing between players.

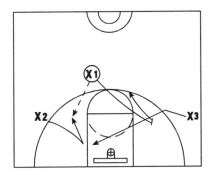

Drill #19: Screen and Roll Drill

Objective: To develop the footwork and screening techniques necessary to execute a screen and roll away from the ball play.

Description: The team should be divided into groups of three. The first group should be positioned as shown in Diagram 19. X1 passes from the point to the wing, X2. X1 then breaks to set a screen for X3. X3 cuts off the screen and looks for a pass, while X1 rolls to the basket. X2 chooses the most open man to which to pass. The coach may also designate which player involved in the screen and roll should receive the pass. The level of difficulty in the drill may be increased by adding one or more defenders to the drill.

Coaching Point:

- The emphasis should be placed on using the proper footwork to execute the screen and roll.

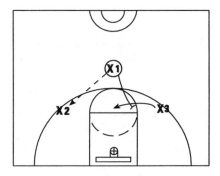

Drill #20: Double Post Screening Drill

Objective: To develop the footwork and screening skills of post players; to practice catching and passing the ball.

Description: This drill requires seven players. Two offensive players and two defenders are positioned at either the high or low post. Three perimeter players take positions at both wings and the point. To begin the drill, the ball is passed to either wing. The ballside post player executes a spin move into the lane to get into position to receive the ball. The wing does not make the pass. After two seconds in the lane, the post player then moves into position to set a screen for the offside post player, who rubs his defender off the screen and breaks into the lane for a pass. The drill should be run at full speed with the ball moving around the perimeter until a pass can be made to a post player breaking off a screen.

Coaching Point:

- The coach should pay special attention to the footwork and screening techniques of both post players, as well as the amount of time spent in the lane.

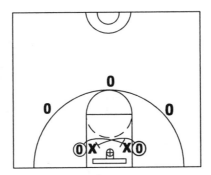

Drill #21: Rub-Off Drill

Objective: To practice setting a back screen; to enhance the ability to cut off a well-set screen.

Description: This drill begins with two players positioned as shown in Diagram A. X1 passes to X2, then moves to set a back screen for X2. X2 jabs to his right against an imaginary defender, then pivots and executes a jab-crossover move. Dribbling with the left hand, X2 rubs his defender off the screen set by X1. In Diagram B, a high post player is added and the two-player game is turned into a split maneuver. After the pass from X1, X2 passes to X3. After the second pass, X1 sets the screen for X2. X2 rubs his defender off the screen, and X1 continues around to the low post.

Coaching Points:

- The coach should stress the importance of setting a good solid screen.
- The emphasis should also be on cutting close to the screen in order to rub off the defender.

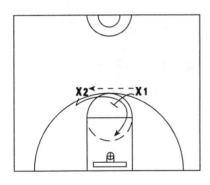

Diagram A

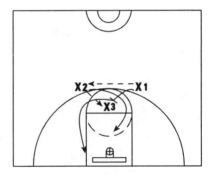

Diagram B

CHAPTER 4

PASSING DRILLS

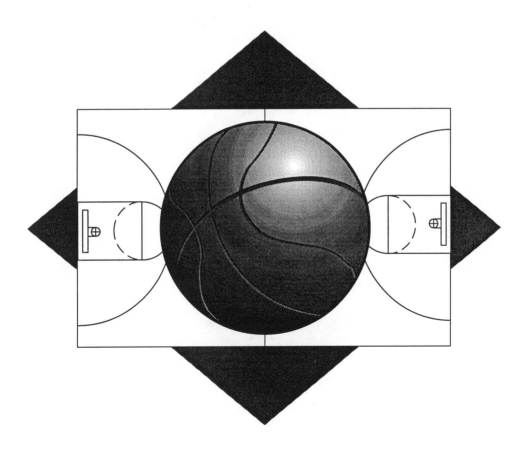

Drill #22: Moving Pairs Passing Drill

Objective: To develop basic skills in passing and receiving the basketball.

Description: The drill involves pairing up the players. Each pair starts the drill with a ball. Initially, one player is without the ball while the other player acts as a passer. The player without the ball executes a good cut to get open and receives the pass with his hands extended in the proper position. The pass is caught in the air and the receiver executes a quick stop, preparing him to become the passer. The drill continues for a time period designated by the coach. As skill levels progress, the coach may wish to include passing off the dribble drive and passing to backdoor cuts to the basket.

Coaching Points:

- The emphasis should be on making good cuts to get open, receiving the ball in the air, and getting in position to make the next pass.
- The coach should also emphasize using proper hand and body position when making or receiving passes and stepping to the pass when receiving it.

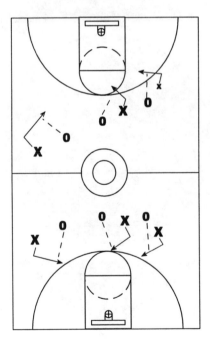

Drill #23: Uncontested Passing Drills

Objective: To develop catching, passing, and ballhandling skills using a variety of techniques.

Description: The players form two lines facing each other approximately four to six feet apart. The first player in one line passes to the player opposite him, who takes one dribble and passes to the next player in the opposite line. The drill continues with the players alternating hands on the dribble for 30 seconds. The players then form a circle and practice behind-the-back passes around the circle. After one revolution, they reverse directions and use the other hand. Alternate-hand and around-the-body passes are practiced in a similar fashion. Lastly, a second ball is introduced. The players then keep both balls in motion around the circle as rapidly as possible.

Coaching Point:

- The emphasis should be on crispness and accuracy of passes and extending hands toward the ball when receiving a pass.

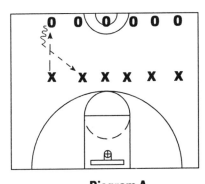

Diagram A

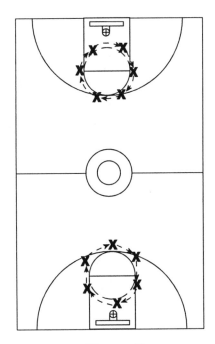

Diagram B

Drill #24: Three-Person Weave

Objective: To practice passing the ball on a three-person weave fast break; to practice maintaining proper court position on the fast break.

Description: The team is divided into as many three-player groups as facilities will accommodate. The first group assumes a position at one endline as shown. On command from the coach, X1 inbounds the ball to X2 and then cuts behind as X2 moves upcourt. X2 then passes the ball to X3 and cuts behind X3. The players move upcourt using a three-player weave. The ball never touches the floor. At the other basket, X2 shoots a lay-up after receiving a pass from X1. X3 rebounds the lay-up.

Coaching Point:

- The player making the pass should always cut behind the player to whom the pass was made.

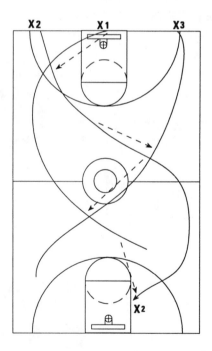

Drill #25: Baseball Pass On the Break

Objective: To develop the ability to throw an accurate baseball pass on the fast break; to practice performing a straight-line fast break.

Description: Three players execute a straight-line fast break. The ball is passed back and forth between the three players, who maintain their respective lanes. The ball is not allowed to touch the floor. X1 shoots the lay-up. X3 rebounds the lay-up, while X2 releases for a fast break. X3 then inbounds the ball to X1, who throws a baseball pass to the breaking X2.

Coaching Point:

- The proper fundamentals and techniques for executing the three-person fast break, as well as throwing the baseball pass, should be emphasized.

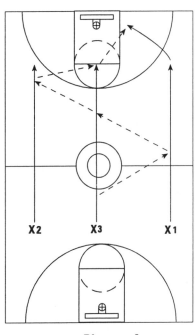

Diagram A

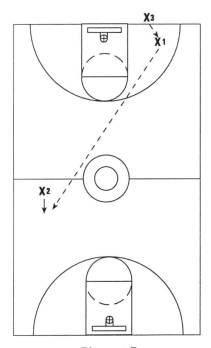

Diagram B

Drill #26: Strongside Three-Player Game

Objective: To develop catching and passing skills; to practice the triangle offense.

Description: Two three-player groups set up on opposite sides of the court. Each group consists of a wing player (F), a guard (G), and a low post player (C). The drill begins with the ball in F's hands. F passes to G and receives a return pass as he moves to the baseline (Diagram A). F then passes into C, who passes back to F as F breaks to the basket (Diagram B). When F passes into the post, he can pivot in the opposite direction and break to the lane, receiving the pass and a screen from C. The difficulty of the drill can be increased by adding three defensive players.

Coaching Point:

• The coach should emphasize the pivot and break to the basket by F, and the accuracy and crispness of all passes.

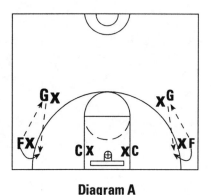

Diagram A

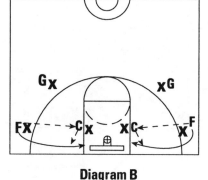

Diagram B

Drill #27: Player on the Spot

Objective: To develop the ability to make accurate bounce passes; to practice defending against the bounce pass.

Description: The players form a six-foot circle. One designated "player on the spot" is in the middle of the circle on defense. The player with the ball must execute a bounce pass to anyone in the circle except the two players adjacent to him. The defender attempts to cut off the pass. When the defender succeeds in intercepting or deflecting a pass, he changes places with the individual who made the pass.

Coaching Points:

- The drill should be run at full speed, emphasizing endurance, footwork, and changing direction on part of the defender.
- Offensive players should practice delivering the ball to a receiver at which the defender is not looking directly.

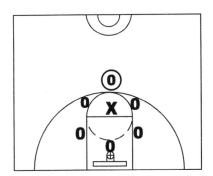

Drill #28: Post Player Bounce Pass Drill

Objective: To develop passing and ballhandling skills in post players.

Description: The coach should have all centers, power forwards, and small forwards rotating into their positions during the drill. The small forward (SF) passes down to the power forward (PF), with the center (C) moving out to the high post area. SF then breaks down through the key looking for a pass. If no pass is forthcoming, SF comes back to the wing, always alert for a late pass. When SF gets open at or near the three-point line, PF finds him with a bounce pass. SF then puts up a three-point jump-shot. The coach can run this drill with no defense, a token defense, or against an aggressive pressure defense.

Coaching Point:

- The emphasis should be on passing to SF when he comes open, either on the cut through the key or on the trip out to the wing.

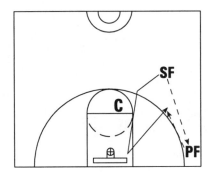

Drill #29: Post Player In the Middle Passing Drill

Objective: To develop passing skills in post players and improve hands, peripheral vision and quickness.

Description: The coach should divide the squad into two groups, with the centers and power forwards split equally between the two. Each group sets up around the key (Diagrams A and B), with one post player in the middle. In Diagram A, the post player begins the drill by passing to the right. The quick passes rotate as shown. In Diagram B, the post player has to handle two live balls in action simultaneously. He may pass to whomever he likes, but must be able to catch the second ball, execute a second pass, and be ready to catch the return of the first pass.

Coaching Point:

* The coach may wish to increase the speed of the drills as skill levels improve.

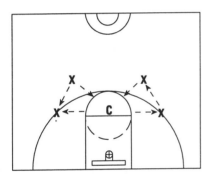

Diagram A

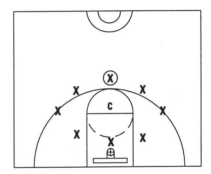

Diagram B

Drill #30: Pass and Rebound Jump-Shot Drill

Objective: To develop the ability to pass, rebound, and shoot baseline jump-shots.

Description: The team should be divided into groups of three. Two groups may run the drill simultaneously, one at each end of the floor. The players are aligned as shown in the diagram below. The guard (G) begins the action by making a good pass to the post player (C). With the pass to the high post, the wing (F) drifts toward the baseline, where he receives a pass from C. F takes the baseline jumper and C crashes the boards, putting any missed shots back up. C then outlets the ball to G. The players then rotate assignments and repeat the drill. The coach may increase the difficulty of the drill by adding one, two, or three defensive players.

Coaching Point:

- The coach should emphasize proper passing, rebounding, and shooting fundamentals.

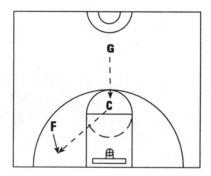

CHAPTER 5

SHOOTING DRILLS

Drill #31: Shooting Warm-Up

Objective: To practice shooting from a variety of positions and angles on the court; to warm-up the muscles, ligaments, tendons, and joints involved in shooting.

Description: This drill involves a coach and a player. The coach begins the drill by passing the ball to the player, who is standing to one side of the basket next to the lane. The player shoots the ball, while the coach rebounds either the missed shot or a made basket. After each rebound, the coach passes the ball back to the player. The player continues to shoot from the same spot until ten shots have been made from that location. The player then moves across the lane to the same spot on the other side of the lane and the process is repeated. Once ten shots have been made from the new spot, the player again moves to the opposite side, this time to a point a few feet farther from the basket. The process is repeated until the player has eventually shot from four locations on each side of the free throw lane.

Coaching Points:

- Proper shooting form and technique should be emphasized.
- The coach can add difficulty by holding a hand in front of the player's face on each shot.

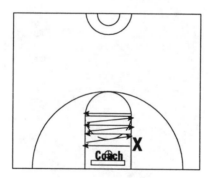

Drill #32: Conditioning Shooting

Objective: To practice shooting; to develop stamina.

Description: Initially, this drill involves one player (X) and a coach. The drill begins when the coach passes the ball to X, who is positioned at the elbow. X shoots a jump-shot and then sprints to touch the far sideline. The coach rebounds the shot attempt. After touching the sideline, X runs to the other elbow, receives another pass from the coach, and quickly shoots a jump-shot. The process is repeated on a non-stop basis until X has made an arbitrary number of jump-shots (e.g., 10). Diagram B illustrates a sequence that involves two players (X1, X2), two coaches, and two basketballs. In this instance, X1 and X2 touch the midcourt line and shoot either elbow or wing jump-shots.

Coaching Points:

- If the drill involves two players simultaneously, competition can be fostered by seeing which player can make ten shots from a given area first.
- Despite the fatiguing aspect of the drill, players should be encouraged to maintain proper shooting form.

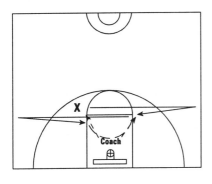

Diagram A

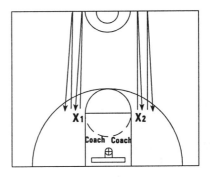

Diagram B

Drill #33: 55-Second Shooting

Objective: To practice shooting under time-intense conditions; to develop stamina.

Description: The drill involves three players—a rebounder (X1), a passer (X2), and a shooter (X3). At least two basketballs are used in the drill. X2 passes the ball to X3. X3 shoots the ball, sprints to touch a cone which has been placed approximately ten feet away, and then retreats to his initial starting position for another shot. X1 rebounds each shot attempt and passes it back to X2. X2 then gets the ball quickly to X3. X3 uses quick movement to get off the shot and tries to take at least 25 shots in the allotted 55 seconds. The position of the cone and the shooter can be varied during the drill to give the shooter practice at shooting from different angles and locations on the court. After a predetermined number of repetitions of the drill, the players switch roles.

Coaching Points:

- A quick release of the shot should be emphasized.
- The rebounder and the passer should efficiently and enthusiastically perform their responsibilities.

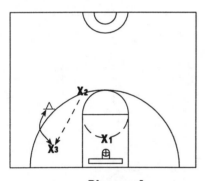

Diagram A

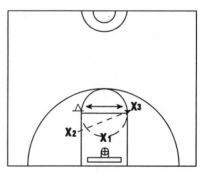

Diagram B

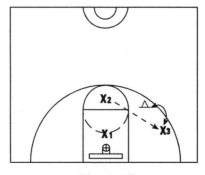

Diagram C

Drill #34: Spot Jump-Shooting Drill

Objective: To improve accuracy in jump-shooting; to improve ball-handling skills; to develop stamina.

Description: A coach or manager should be designated as a timekeeper/recorder. The players shoot 25 jump-shots in this drill, five shots from each of five designated areas on the floor. On the timekeeper's command, the player takes his first shot from the first area. He runs to get his rebound and dribbles back to the same area for the second shot. After completing five shots, the player moves on to the second area and so on. The timekeeper/recorder keeps track of the number of shots made in each area and records the total time necessary to take the 25 shots.

Coaching Point:

- The coach should chart and post each player's results so that players can follow their progress in both accuracy and speed.

Drill #35: Speed Shooting Jump-Shot Drill

Objective: To improve proficiency in jump-shooting, emphasizing a quick release off the pass.

Description: The drill involves two pkayers—a shooter (O) and a rebounder/passer (X). Eight spots should be designated in an arc around the basket as shown in the diagram below. A coach should be designated as a timekeeper. Player O takes a position just inside the three-point line near either baseline, while X is under the basket. X begins the drill by passing crisply to the shooter, who releases the first jump-shot. O immediately moves to the next designated spot around the perimeter, receives a pass, shoots, and moves on. The coach/timekeeper designates whent o start and finish the drill. The drill can also be adapted to jump-shots or set shots taken outside the three-point line. To increase the difficulty level of the drill, a defensive player can be added to keep a hand in the shooter's face.

Coaching Points:

- The coach should set the time allowed for completing the drill according to the level of the players he is coaching. Two minutes is usually suitable for high school players.
- The coach may award two points per basket and record scores to stimulate competition.
- The coach should create unity between the two players involved by placing as much emphasis on a crisp accurate pass, as on the shot that follows.

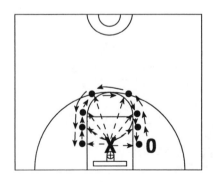

Drill #36: Inside-Outside Screen Jump-Shot Drill

Objective: To teach players the proper techniques to execute a pass inside to the post, a screen for a third player, and a shot off the split maneuver.

Description: The drill is set up with a post player (C) on each side of the lane and two perimeter players (F and G) working with each post player. The perimeter players should be separated from each other and from the post player by at least ten feet. F passes into the post, then moves to set a screen for G. G breaks off the screen, receives a pass from the post, and takes a jump-shot. Perimeter players rotate so that they also have the opportunity to shoot and set screens.

Coaching Points:

- The coach can change the drill by adding defensive players at every position and varying the intensity of the defense being played.
- The emphasis should be placed on setting a good screen and maintaining proper position while screening.

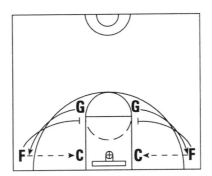

Drill #37: Three-Man Triangle Drill

Objective: To teach players to run a three-man game based on the triangle offense; to practice the shots available in a triangle offense.

Description: The team should be split into groups of three. The first group is positioned as shown in Diagram A. The player with the ball passes across the foul line and breaks down to set a screen for the low post player. After screening, he then breaks across the lane, receiving a pass if he is open or positioning himself on the other side of the lane if he is not. The process is repeated to run the triangle offense (Diagram B); the players take shots as opportunities occur.

Coaching Points:

- The coach should emphasize good screening techniques and the importance of clearing the side of the lane.
- The emphasis should be on taking the shots most likely to present themselves: the jump-shot from the side of the lane after receiving a pass and the drive to the hoop when a side is cleared.

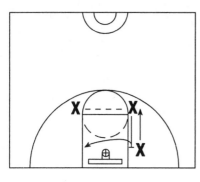

Diagram A

Diagram B

Drill #38: Two-Player Team Shooting Drill

Objective: To enhance conditioning levels; to practice shooting, passing, catching, and offensive rebounding in a competitive atmosphere.

Description: The drill begins with X1 under the basket in a rebounding position with a ball. X2 works to get open, calls for the ball by shouting X1's name, receives the pass, and takes the shot. X2 then crashes the boards to rebound his own shot. If the shot is missed, X2 gets the rebound and keeps shooting until the basket is made. Immediately after passing, X1 moves to another spot. As soon as X2 scores and has possession of the ball, X1 moves to get open and the drill is repeated. Instead of rotating after each basket, the coach may choose to have the players stay in the same positions until the shooter makes an arbitrary number of shots before the players reverse their roles. The coach may add various degrees of defensive pressure on the shooter for realism.

Coaching Points:

- The coach should stress the necessity of communication between the players.
- The emphasis should be on quick execution and sharp movements; however, the players should not sacrifice precision for haste.

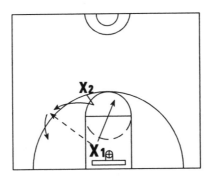

Drill #39: Three-Pass Team Shooting Drill

Objective: To enhance conditioning levels; to practice shooting, passing, catching, and offensive rebounding in a competitive atmosphere.

Description: The drill begins with X1 under the basket in a rebounding position with the ball. X1 hits X2 with an outlet pass and slides into a post position. X2 dribbles to the same side and passes in to the post. X2 then cuts sharply to get open for a return pass from the post and takes the shot. He then crashes the boards and gets the rebound, continuing to shoot until a basket is made. After making the last pass, X1 works outside, ready to move to receive an outlet pass when X2 secures possession. The coach may add varying degrees of defensive pressure on the shooter for realism.

Coaching Point:

- The emphasis should be placed on quick execution and sharp movements to the ball; however, precision should not be sacrificed for haste.

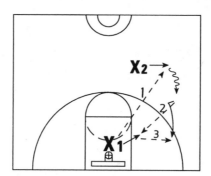

Drill #40: Team Jump-Shot Competition

Objective: To practice jump-shots from the foul line and both corners; to enhance conditioning levels.

Description: The team is divided into groups of three. One group is positioned as shown in the diagram below. Each player has a basketball. Each player shoots jumpers until the three-player team has made a designated number of jump-shots (e.g., 15). As many three-player teams participate at a time as there are half-courts and basketballs available. Instead of requiring a fixed number of shots, the coach may also decide to run the drill for a specified amount of time.

Coaching Point:

- The emphasis should be placed on the speed with which each player retrieves his own shot and returns to his spot on the floor.

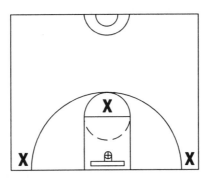

Drill #41: Hook-Shot Proficiency Drill

Objective: To practice shooting right-and left-handed hook shots; to enhance conditioning levels.

Description: This drill begins with a player standing inside the foul lane to the right of the basket. The player takes a right-handed hook shot and tries to catch the ball before it hits the floor. He then maneuvers to the left side of the basket, taking a left-handed hook shot, again trying to catch the ball before it hits the floor. The drill may run until the player makes a prescribed number of shots or for a set period of time.

Coaching Points:

- The coach should emphasize the proper footwork: jumping off the left foot when taking a right-handed hook shot and the right foot when taking a left-handed hook shot.
- The player should practice keeping the ball above his shoulders.

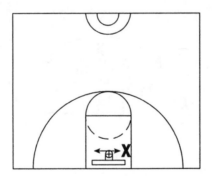

Drill #42: Power Hook Shot Drill

Objective: To develop a power move into the lane leading to a short hook shot.

Description: The players should be grouped in pairs. X1 passes the ball to X2 at the free throw lane. X2 meets the pass and dribbles down the right side of the key, then uses a spin-off dribble, changes to a left-hand dribble, and powers into the key for a left-hand hook shot. He rebounds his own shot and passes back to X1 to continue the drill. Five shots are taken, and then the drill is reversed to the left side of the key. X2 drives down the left side of the lane, uses a spin-off dribble, changes to a right-hand dribble, and powers into the key for a right-hand hook shot. He then rebounds his own shot and passes out to X1. After the shooter has taken five shots from each side, the passer and the shooter switch roles.

Coaching Point:

- The emphasis should be placed on using the proper footwork for the foot plant leading to the spin-off dribble and the power action into the key.

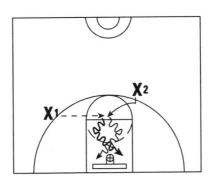

Drill #43: Caveman Drill

Objective: To instill physical and mental toughness; to develop aggressive scoring skills.

Description: The players are grouped into pairs. One pair begins the drill under the basket (Diagram A). Extraordinarily excessive physical contact (i.e., slugging the other player) is an example of the only type of action not allowed in this drill. The offensive player does everything he can in order to score. The drill can be expanded to half-court, three-on-three competition with the defense picking up the pressure at either the foul line or at midcourt (Diagram B).

Coaching Point:

- The emphasis should be on aggressive offensive play under the basket.

Diagram A

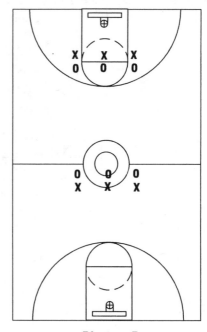

Diagram B

Drill #44: Two-Player Perimeter Shooting Drill

Objective: To practice shooting the ball from a variety of offensive moves; to develop stamina.

Description: The players should be grouped in pairs, one working at a basket at a time. The shooter takes a total of 25 shots as he moves around the perimeter. The rebounder passes the ball back out to his teammate as quickly as possible after each shot. The first ten shots are taken without a dribble. The player takes one dribble on the next five shots, and two dribbles on the five after that. The last five shots must be taken off a spin or crossover dribble. The coach may decide to vary the offensive moves and the order in which they are used. He may also decide to run the drill for a specified amount of time instead of a certain number of shots.

Coaching Points:

- The rebounder should concentrate making crisp, accurate passes.
- Emphasis should be on using the proper footwork and techniques to perform the various offensive moves.

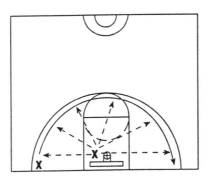

Drill #45: Shooting on the Spot

Objective: To practice shooting from different areas of the court.

Description: The team is divided into two groups, with one group positioned at each end of the court as shown in the diagram below. All of the players from a group begin at Spot 1. The first player for each team has a basketball. On the coach's signal, the player takes a shot from Spot 1. If he makes the shot, he gets his own rebound and dribbles to the next spot on the floor and so on. If he misses, he gets the rebound and begins again from Spot 1. The winner is the first team to have all players complete the trip around the perimeter. The coach may also decide to run the drill for a specified amount of time. In that case, a player who misses his shot retrieves the ball and passes to the next player on the team. After the time is up, the winner is the team that has made the most baskets.

Coaching Point:

• The emphasis should be on working quickly, while maintaining good shooting form and using proper techniques.

Drill #46: Quick-Thinking Drill

Objective: To practice responding quickly to take a shot.

Description: A player stands under the basket with his back to the coach. The coach rolls the basketball toward the lane and yells "Ball." When the coach yells "Ball," the player turns and goes after the ball. As the player reaches the ball and picks it up, the coach gives his next direction by calling out "Jumper" or "Lay-up." The player must execute whichever shot the coach signals. The coach should roll the player a set number of balls before the next player takes his place. Penalties may be assessed for not following the coach's commands correctly.

Coaching Point:

- The coach should emphasize the importance of reacting quickly but correctly to commands.

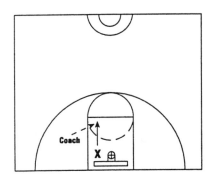

Drill #47: Wing Play

Objective: To practice shooting skills when confronted with a close-out move by a defender.

Description: The drill involves either two players or one player and a coach. One of the players serves as an offensive player (X) and is positioned on the wing with a ball. The other player (or coach) acts as a defensive player. The defender rotates to the ball and attempts to close out (i.e., "shut down") the offensive player. Diagrams A-D illustrate four possible reactions the offensive player can use against the close-out: shoot a jump-shot (A); take one or two dribbles and then shoot a jump-shot (B); shoot a runner to the basket (C); and perform a crossover move and then shoot a jump-shot (D). Players should practice all four options.

Coaching Point:

- Regardless of the move executed to counter the close-out, offensive players should always adhere to proper shooting techniques and fundamentals.

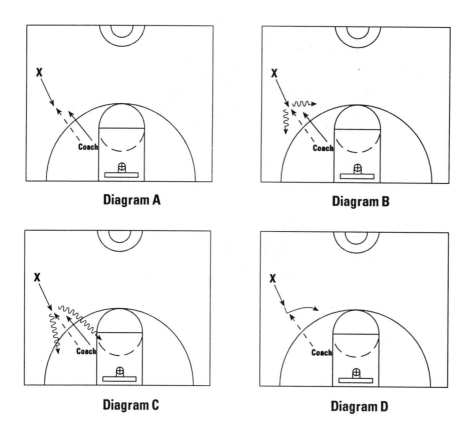

Diagram A   **Diagram B**

Diagram C   **Diagram D**

Drill #48: Back Screen Options

Objective: To practice shooting after executing an offensive move off of a back screen.

Description: The drill involves two offensive players and two coaches. The drill starts with one player on the wing and one player in the low post area. The coaches, each with a ball, are in the front court area. On command from the coach, the low post player comes up and sets a back screen for the player on the wing. Diagrams A-C illustrate three of the primary options available to the wing player: pop out, receive a pass, and shoot (A); fade, step to the ball, receive a pass, and shoot (B); and slip the screen, pop out, receive a pass, and shoot (C). Regardless of the option the wing player chooses, one of the coaches passes to the wing, who then shoots. The other coach reacts to the actions of the low post player and passes the ball to that player, who then takes the shot.

Coaching Points:

- The proper techniques for setting a back screen should be followed.
- Two players can be used as passers in the drill instead of the two coaches.

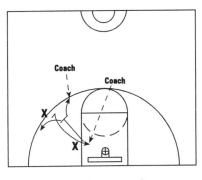

Diagram A

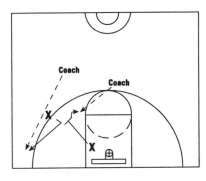

Diagram B

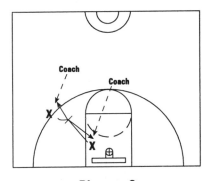

Diagram C

Drill #49: Combination Drill

Objective: To practice shooting off of a post-up move; to practice flashing out to receive a pass to set up a shot.

Description: The drill involves one coach with two basketballs, a shooter (X1), and a screener (X2). X1 begins the drill by making a post-up move in the block. The coach then passes inside to X1, who shoots. X1 then flashes out to the free throw line, breaks off a screen set by X2, receives another pass from the coach, and shoots a jump-shot. This sequence is illustrated in Diagram A. Diagram B shows a second option. In this situation, X2 sets a screen. X1 breaks off the screen, receives a pass from the coach, and shoots a jump-shot. X2 then sets a second screen. X1 comes off the screen, flashes to the wing, receives a pass from the coach, and takes a good shot.

Coaching Points:

- Proper shooting techniques and fundamentals should be emphasized.
- The proper steps for executing a pindown should be followed.

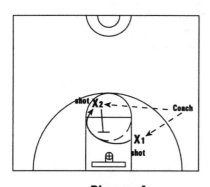

Diagram A

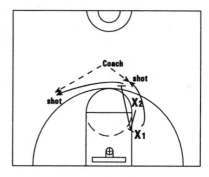

Diagram B

Drill #50: Moves Off the Dribble

Objective: To practice shooting after making a move off the dribble.

Description: The drill involves a coach and a player. The drill begins with the player at the midcourt line. He then speed dribbles to the top of the key. The coach steps up to challenge the player, who executes a crossover move, takes one dribble, and shoots a jump-shot.

Coaching Points:

- Variety can be added to the drill by having the player execute other moves instead of crossover moves (e.g., hesitation, spin, etc.).
- Players should adhere to the proper techniques and fundamentals for shooting.

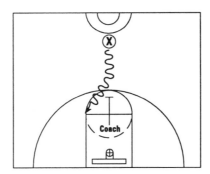

Drill #51: Two-Ball Pindowns

Objective: To practice shooting off a screen; to learn to read the actions of a player setting a pick; to practice pindown moves.

Description: The drill involves two coaches (each with a basketball) and two players: a picker on the wing (X1) and a player in the low post (X2). The drill begins with X1 making a pindown move in the block. X2 reads the actions of the picker and reacts accordingly. Diagrams A-D illustrate four options for X2 off the pindown. The coaches pass the ball to the closest player to them once X1 and X2 have made their moves.

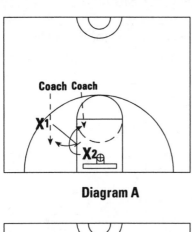

Diagram A

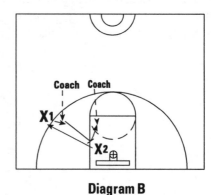

Diagram B

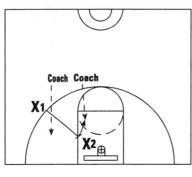

Diagram C

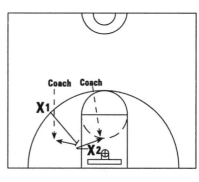

Diagram D

Drill #52: Two-Ball Bigs and Littles

Objective: To practice moves and shooting off a pick; to develop the ability to read the actions of a teammate.

Description: This drill involves two coaches, a post player (X1), and a guard (X2). X1 sets a pick for X2. X1 and X2 must read each other's actions. If X2 goes up, X1 replaces X2 in the box. If X2 uses X1 as a picker and goes down, X1 goes up. Diagrams A-D illustrate two versions of two separate options. Once X1 and X2 have made their moves, the two coaches pass to both players for shots.

Coaching Points:

- Players should set good picks and screens.
- Proper shooting techniques and fundamentals should be emphasized.

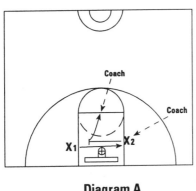

Diagram A

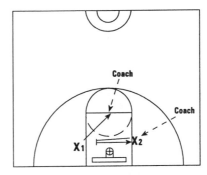

Diagram B

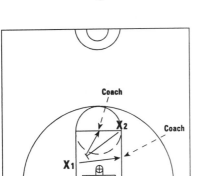

Diagram C

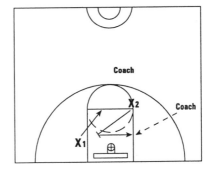

Diagram D

Drill #53: Reverse Dribble Backboard Shot

Objective: To practice using the backboard on a jump-shot; to develop the ability to reverse dribble.

Description: The drill initially involves one player (X) and a coach. The coach assumes a stationary guarding position adjacent to the low post area. X starts the drill on the wing and dribbles to the coach. He assumes that the defender will beat him to the baseline to prevent the jump-shot. Once X reaches the coach, he pulls the ball around for a reverse dribble, takes one large step, and shoots a bank shot. The player gets the rebound and goes to the other side of the floor to repeat the drill.

Coaching Point:

- The coach can add variety and difficulty to the drill by incorporating a defender to apply pressure defense against the offensive player.

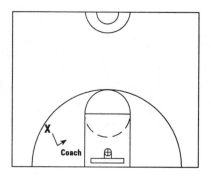

Drill #54: Pick and Roll

Objective: To practice shooting off the pick and roll move; to develop passing skills.

Description: Initially, the drill involves two players (X1, X2) and a coach. The coach has two basketballs. The drill starts when X1 sets a pick for X2. X2 breaks off the pick, receives a pass from the coach, and shoots a jump-shot. X1 subsequently rolls to the basket, gets a pass from the coach, and shoots. Once the players have mastered the basic pick and roll move and shot, a third player (X3), another coach, and a third basketball can be added. Diagram B illustrates one possible sequence for the three-ball version of the pick and roll drill. X1 sets a pick for X2 and then rolls to the basket. The coach passes to X1, who shoots. X2 comes off the pick by X1, gets a pass from the coach, and then passes the ball to X3 in the corner for a shot. After making the pass, X2 continues across the key, receives a pass from the coach, and shoots a jump-shot.

Coaching Point:

- Proper shooting techniques and fundamentals should be emphasized.

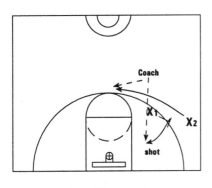

Diagram A

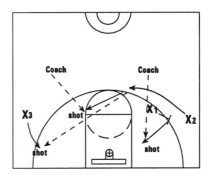

Diagram B

Drill #55: No Basket Jump Shots

Objective: To develop proper jump-shooting form.

Description: Players form two lines facing each other approximately ten feet apart. Each player has a basketball. The players practice shooting the ball to each other, concentrating on using proper jump-shooting technique.

Coaching Point:

• The coach should circulate among the players correcting any errors in form and paying special attention to the concentration level of the players.

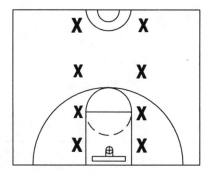

Drill #56: Concentration Jump-Shot Drill

Objective: To improve a player's confidence in shooting jump-shots.

Description: The players assume a position near either baseline 12 to 15 feet from the basket. They concentrate on the rim and go through the motions of shooting a proper jump-shot without a ball. The players should concentrate and visualize each shot. They should have a mental image of the ball going in the basket. Players should rotate in an arc to five positions around the perimeter, remaining 12 to 15 feet from the rim.

Coaching Point:

- The coach should observe each player's concentration level carefully and adjust the time period allowed for the drill accordingly.

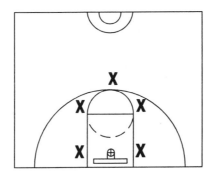

Drill #57: Rotation Shooting Drill

Objective: To allow a team to take a large number of shots from different areas on the floor.

Description: The team is divided into four equal groups which form lines as shown in the diagram below. The first player in each line takes a practice shot, gets his own rebound, and passes to the next player in his line. The player then rotates in a clockwise direction to the end of the next line.

Coaching Point:

- The coach may wish to vary this drill by adding a fifth station at the foul line.

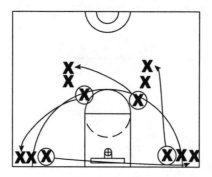

CHAPTER 6

FAST-BREAK DRILLS

Drill #58: Three-Player Fast-Break

Objective: To develop players' rebounding, outlet passing, and baseball passing skills.

Description: The coach should divide the squad into groups of three players and position the first group along the baseline as shown in the diagram below. The ball starts with the right wing (X1), who begins the drill with a pass to the middle (X2). X2 passes to the opposite wing (X3), then sprints upcourt and receives a return pass from X3 about midcourt. While X1 and X3 sprint wide upcourt and then cut sharply to the basket, X2 dribbles to the foul line and stops penetration. He bounce passes to either wing for the lay-up and moves into position to receive an outlet pass on the side the shooter vacated. The opposite wing rebounds and makes an outlet pass to X2, who then makes a fullcourt baseball pass to the right wing player in the next group of three. The coach may add difficulty to the drill by having shooters use their weaker hand while shooting.

Coaching Point:

- The drill should be run at full speed, emphasizing spacing, passing, and cutting sharply to the basket.

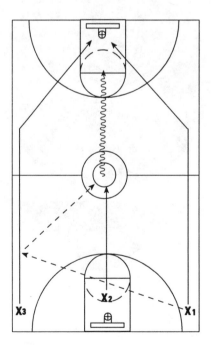

Drill #59: Fill the Lane, No-Bounce Fast-Break Drill

Objective: To develop fundamental fast-break skills.

Description: The coach should divide the squad into three-player groups. Player X1 has the ball in the center of the court. Players X2 and X3 position themselves as wide wings, close to the sidelines. X1 passes to X3 and sprints upcourt in his lane to receive a return pass. X1 then dribbles to the foul line and passes to X2, cutting hard to the basket for a lay-up. All three players crash the boards. For the return trip, X1 fills X3's lane, X2 assumes X1's original role, and X3 replaces X2. The group makes three fast-breaks down the court, with the players rotating into every role. The level of difficulty of the drill can be increased by forcing the shooters to use their weaker hand.

Coaching Point:

- The drill should be run at full speed with emphasis placed on spacing, passing, and cutting sharply to the basket.

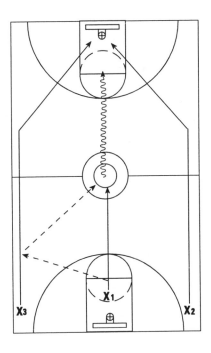

Drill #60: Five-Player Fast-Break

Objective: To develop team fast-break skills, to enhance stamina levels.

Description: The coach should divide the squad into teams of five players. Each team should have a player act as the ballhandler. The players are positioned as shown in the diagram below. PF is responsible for rebounding and inbounding after each basket. To begin the drill, PF inbounds the ball to C, who passes to the ballhandler, PG. PG then speed dribbles upcourt with the other players filling the lanes as shown. As PG approaches the foul line, the wings cut sharply to the basket and PG feeds any of the four trailers for a lay-up or pull up jump-shot. The drill can continue for a set period of time or until a prescribed number of baskets has been made.

Coaching Points:

- The drill should be run at full speed to gain maximum conditioning benefits.
- The emphasis should be on players hustling to their respective spots on the floor after each basket.

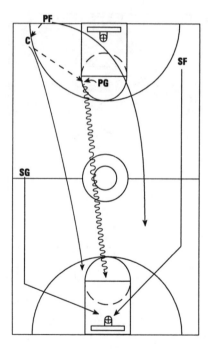

Drill #61: Rebound-Outlet Pass Drill

Objective: To teach proper techniques in rebounding, footwork, and outlet passing.

Description: Four players line up about six feet in front of the basket. A fifth player stands off to either side with the ball. This player shoots a shot off the backboard. The first player in line rebounds the missed shot, lands, and immediately pivots toward the closest sideline, ready to pass. The player should always pivot away from the congestion under the basket and in the middle. As skill levels progress, the coach should add a sixth player near the sideline around midcourt. When the player comes down with the rebound, he pivots and passes to the outlet receiver. To increase the reality level of the drill, the coach can add a seventh player assigned to pressure the outlet pass.

Coaching Points:

- The emphasis should be placed on proper body positioning and footwork.
- More experienced players should work on pivoting in the air so they land facing the near sideline.

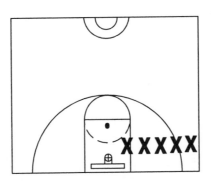

Drill #62: Rebound Two-Pass Fast-Break Drill

Objective: To develop skills in rebounding, outlet passing, and secondary passing.

Description: The team is divided into groups of four with the players positioned as shown in the diagram below. The free throw shooter puts up an errant shot and plays loose defense on the rebounder. The rebounder secures the ball, pivots toward the near sideline in the air, and executes an outlet pass to the player breaking down the near sideline. The other fast-break player sprints upcourt. As that player crosses midcourt, he cuts toward the receiver of the outlet pass. The outlet receiver hits the cutting player with a pass as he crosses the midcourt line near the center of the court. A fifth player can be added to the drill as a second rebounder. The player not rebounding sprints upcourt to fill the lane left by the player who assumed the middle position in the break. The drill should be continued to the far free throw line, with the wings cutting to the basket for a pass or the middle player pulling up for a short jump-shot.

Coaching Points:

- The emphasis should be on hitting the receiver of the outlet pass in full stride as he progresses upcourt.
- The coach should stress to the cutter to time his move to the center of the midcourt line so he arrives at the same time as the pass.
- There should be no delay in making or receiving passes; the ball should never hit the floor.

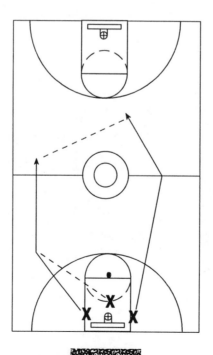

Drill #63: Fast-Break Bounce Pass Feed Drill

Objective: To develop bounce pass skills while hitting a wing cutting to the basket off the fast-break.

Description: This drill begins with three players spread out near the midcourt line. The middle player dribbles toward the foul line at full speed, while both wings break hard to the basket once they reach the foul line extended. The dribbler then feeds one of the wings with a bounce pass as they go in for the lay-up. The coach may also add a defensive player assigned to pick up the ballhandler at the free throw line.

Coaching Points:

- The emphasis should be on passing technique and accuracy.
- Players should practice making the bounce pass with both hands.

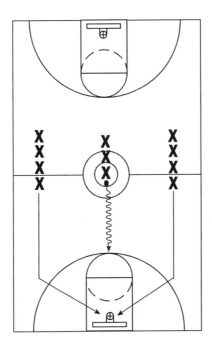

Drill #64: Quick Decision Fast-Break Drill

Objective: To develop the ability of players leading a fast-break to make decisions about where to distribute the ball.

Description: The coach may divide the squad into five-player groups or station two players permanently on defense and form three-player offensive teams with the rest. The two defenders take tandem positions at the free throw line and baseline. The offensive players begin at midcourt. The middle player dribbles toward the foul line at full speed, with the wings cutting to the basket. If the ballhandler is picked up aggressively by the front defender, he passes to either wing. If the front defender sags to prevent a pass to one wing, the dribbler passes to the other wing or pulls up for a short jump-shot. The ballhandler may also choose to drive by the front defender, creating a three-on-one situation.

Coaching Point:

• The coach should observe the ballhandler's decision and stop the drill to make corrections if needed.

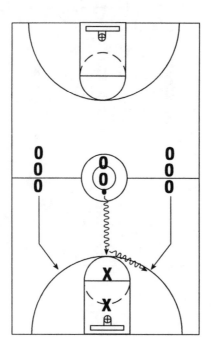

Drill #65: Outlet Pass Options Drill

Objective: To practice rebounding and outlet pass skills, to improve the ability to recognize options as they develop.

Description: Groups of three players should be positioned as shown in Diagram A. A coach or manager stands near the free throw line and throws up an errant shot. X1 grabs the rebound and attempts to hit X2 with a baseball pass in an imaginary outlet box (Diagram A). X2 and X3 both release downcourt. In Diagram B, X2 breaks toward X1 to receive the outlet pass, then passes the ball to X3, who takes it downcourt. A third option is illustrated in Diagram C. X2 breaks toward the rebounder to receive the pass, stops sharply, and pivots back downcourt, filling the outside lane. X1 passes to X3 on the opposite wing, who speed dribbles across the midcourt line. The coach may choose to add three defenders to the drill to offer token resistance by putting their hands in the offensive players' faces and cutting off passing lanes. The defensive intensity should be increased as the players' level of proficiency improves.

Coaching Point:

- The coach should stress proper rebounding position, footwork, and, if possible, pivoting in the air. The rebounder should be encouraged to snap the ball down sharply and follow with a quick, crisp outlet pass.

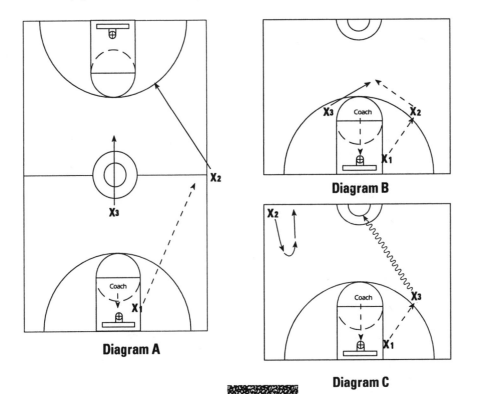

Diagram A

Diagram B

Diagram C

Drill #66: Middle Fast-Break Options Drill

Objective: To increase proficiency in executing a fast-break; to learn to recognize options as they present themselves.

Description: The drill begins with three offensive players aligned at midcourt, with the ball in X1's hands. (Diagram A). As X1 nears the top of the key, the wings exercise a crossing maneuver with X2 setting a screen for X3 in the low post area. X3 scrapes off his defender and pops out to the edge of the lane for a pass from X1. In Diagram B, X1 passes to X2 and then screens away for X3, who breaks off the screen to receive a pass from X2 and take a jump-shot. The coach may add two additional offensive players and fill all the lanes (Diagram C). In that case, X1 can pass to either wing or hit a trailer. He may also hit a wing coming off a screen by one of his teammates.

Coaching Point:

- The emphasis should be placed on keeping players wide to the sidelines.

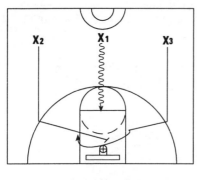

Diagram A

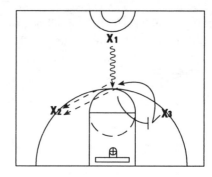

Diagram B

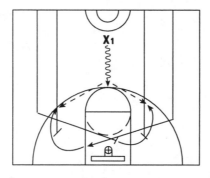

Diagram C

Drill #67: Fast-Break Three-Point Shot Drill

Objective: To develop fast-break skills utilizing two- and three-point scoring options in a competitive situation.

Description: The coach should divide the squad into three teams of five. Team A moves upcourt on a fast-break with Team B dropping back to play defense. Player A1 leads upcourt, breaking to the basket and cutting back beyond the three-point line as A2 approaches the top of the key with the ball. A3 and A4 fill their lanes and A5 trails as a safety. Team B is positioned on defense as shown in Diagram A. As A1 approaches the top of the key, B1 and B2 race to the midcourt line and return quickly to aggressive defensive positions (Diagram B). During this action, Team C positions itself on the other end of the court to play defense when Team B gets the ball. While B1 and B2 race to midcourt and back, Team A may execute a two-point fast-break utilizing any available option. Once B1 and B2 return, A2 passes out beyond the three-point line to A1 for the three-point shot. A1 may use a reverse or lob pass if he is unable to take the shot.

Coaching Point:

- The coach should emphasize getting the quick two-point fast-break if available, and, if not, getting off a quick three-point shot. Ball movement and shot selection should also be emphasized.

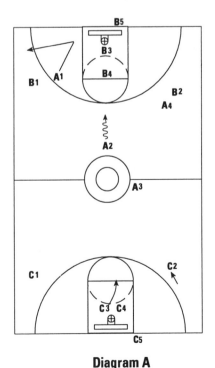

Diagram A

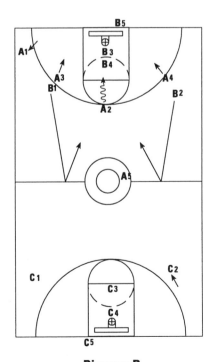

Diagram B

Drill #68: Fast-Break Against the Press Drill

Objective: To develop the team's ability to execute a fast-break; to practice breaking the press.

Description: The coach should divide the squad into five-player teams. The drill is initially run without a defense on the floor. The players rebound a shot and practice moving the ball up the floor as described in previous drills or according to the team's own fast-break system. They work until a basket is made, and then all five players hustle past the end line. On the return trip, they practice offensive systems designed to break various fullcourt presses. The next group of five then moves in and repeats the process. The drill may also be run with five defenders on the floor. The level of defensive intensity should increase as the players' level of proficiency increases.

Coaching Points:

- The players should run the drill at full speed and hustle to their designated positions at each end of the floor.
- The emphasis should be on passing the ball upcourt, coming to meet the pass, and looking upcourt for the next pass.

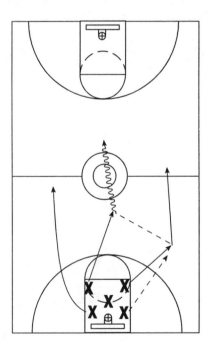

Drill #69: Four-On-Four-On-Four

Objective: To improve the basic techniques involved in fast-breaking.

Description: The drill is performed with three four-person teams. Initially, a four-on-two break is conducted. Two additional defenders, who have been off the court on the sideline, come together at the center jump circle after the ball has passed the half-court line. At that point, four-on-four competition exists. The offensive team attempts to score. Once the defensive team gets the rebound, they break to the other basket on offense against the third team. The new defensive team goes from a two-person defense to a four-person defense in the same manner as the original defenders.

Coaching Point:

- Different points of emphasis for the drill can be made by assigning specific point-scoring values to particular actions (e.g., one point for an offensive rebound, one point for a turnover, etc.)

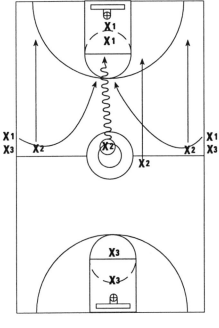

Diagram A

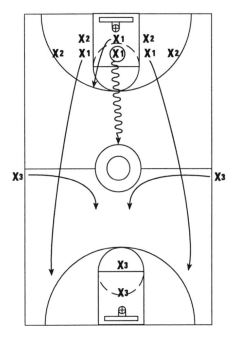

Diagram B

Drill #70: Five-On-Three Competitive Break

Objective: To practice scoring in a fast-break situation against limited pressure; to practice shooting free throws.

Description: The drill involves two five-player teams. The drill begins with one player from Team A shooting a foul shot. If the foul shot is missed, all three of Team A's players closest to the basket attempt to get the rebound and score. If the foul shot is made, Team A is awarded one point and Team B gets the ball out of bounds. Team B then fast-breaks to the other basket. The two members of Team A that were positioned on the lane while the free throw was being shot contest the outlet pass but do not retreat to play defense. At that point, Team B is executing a five-on-three fast-break. If Team B scores a basket, the team is awarded two points. If a team member is fouled, that player takes the line and the process is repeated.

Coaching Point:

- The drill continues for a specific time period (e.g., five minutes) or until one team scores a predetermined number of points.

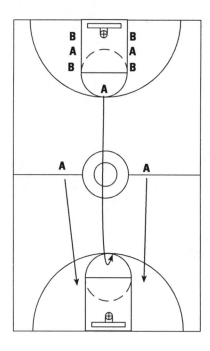

CHAPTER 7

LAY-UP
DRILLS

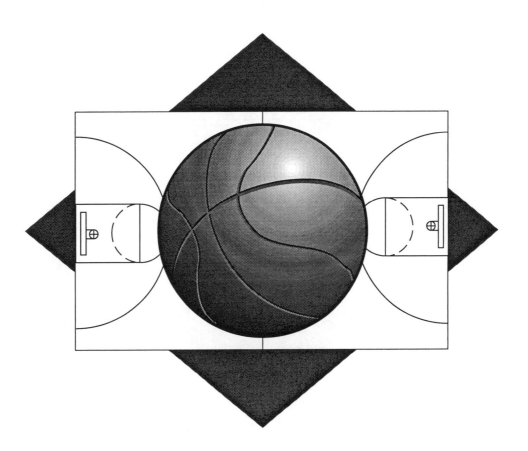

Drill #71: Lay-Up Proficiency Drill

Objective: To practice shooting right- and left-handed lay-ups, to develop stamina.

Description: The drill begins with the player standing inside the lane to the right of the basket. The player shoots a right-handed lay-up and catches the ball before it hits the floor. The player then maneuvers to the left side of the basket, shooting a left-handed lay-up and again catching the ball before it hits the floor. The duration of the drill can be measured by making a prescribed number of lay-ups or by running the drill for a set period of time.

Coaching Points:

- The coach should emphasize using proper footwork, with players jumping off their left foot when taking a right-handed lay-up and off their right foot on a left-handed lay-up.
- The player should practice keeping the ball above his shoulders.
- Variety can be added to the drill by having the players shoot reverse lay-ups with either hand.

Drill #72: Make-It, Take-It Lay-Up Drill

Objective: To develop lay-up shooting skills, emphasizing covering the greatest distance possible with a lay-up scoring move.

Description: The players in this drill initiate dribble-drive lay-up moves from the top of the key, each hash mark, and both baseline corners. Players must complete the move using only one dribble, and make three consecutive shots from each spot on the court. After three consecutive shots are made from a spot, the player moves to the free throw line, where he must make a predetermined percentage of shots before he moves on to the next spot on the floor. The drill continues until the players make all the required shots.

Coaching Points:

- All moves should be made consecutively, without rest, to simulate game conditions as closely as possible.
- The starting points for the lay-up moves and the percentage of made free-throws should be adjusted to fit the age and skill level of the players.

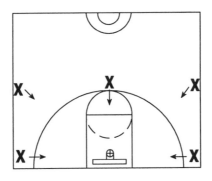

Drill #73: Three-Player Lay-Up Drill

Objective: To develop passing and lay-up skills.

Description: The players form three lines near the half-court line as shown in the diagram below. X2 passes to X1 and then rotates to the sideline. X3 breaks for the basket, receives a pass from X1, and shoots a lay-up. X1 rebounds the shot and passes to X2 for the lay-up. X1 goes to the opposite sideline while X3 rebounds. To complete the rotation, X3 passes to X1 for the lay-up with X2 rebounding. The players then go to the end of different lines.

Coaching Point:

• The emphasis should be on shooting the lay-up off the pass without putting the ball on the floor and on keeping the ball above the shoulders.

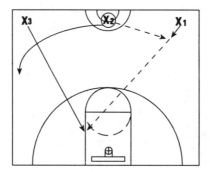

Drill #74: Post Pass Lay-Up Drill

Objective: To practice passing and lay-up skills in a warm-up setting.

Description: Two players (X1, X2) are positioned just outside either elbow of the lane. The other players form lines behind X3 and X4. X3 and X4 begin the drill by dribbling to their outside and passing in to their respective high post player. X3 then cuts through the lane with X4 cutting right off his heels. Each player receives a pass from the opposite post and executes a lay-up. X3 and X4 retrieve their own rebounds and return to the end of the opposite line.

Coaching Points:

- The emphasis should be on making sharp cuts and covering as much distance as possible on the final step to the basket.
- The coach should rotate post players after each has made five to ten passes.

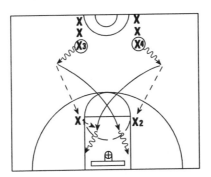

Drill #75: Speed Dribble Lay-Up Drill

Objective: To develop lay-up and dribbling skills; to enhance conditioning level.

Description: The coach should divide the squad into two teams. The teams are placed at opposite baskets as shown in the diagram below. On the whistle, the first player in each line makes a lay-up at his own end of the floor and speed dribbles to the far end of the court, where he shoots another lay-up. He then speed dribbles back down the court and executes a third lay-up at his own basket. The next player in line repeats the same procedure until a designated number of lay-ups (e.g., 15, 20, etc.) has been made by the team. This drill involves speed competition which ends when a team reaches the specified number.

Coaching Point:

- The coach can increase the level of conditioning the drill provides by increasing the designated winning number and/or making the losing team perform calisthenics.

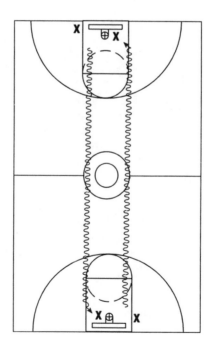

Drill #76: Speed Outlet Lay-Up Drill

Objective: To develop passing, dribbling, and lay-up skills under full-speed competitive conditions.

Description: The coach divides the squad into two teams. Player X1 begins the drill with the ball. Players X2 and X3 are positioned as shown in the diagram below to receive and make outlet passes. At the whistle, X1 makes a lay-up, rebounds, and hits X2 with an outlet pass. X1 then sprints full court while X2 is passing to X3. X3 then feeds X1 the long ball for another lay-up. X3 rebounds and throws the long pass to X1 for a third lay-up at the original end of the court. X3 follows X1 downcourt and both players join the end of the line. X2 takes X3's position. The first player in line takes X2's spot, while the next takes X1's place. The first team to make a predetermined number of lay-ups wins.

Coaching Point:

- The coach should vary the number of lay-ups necessary to win according to the level of conditioning desired.

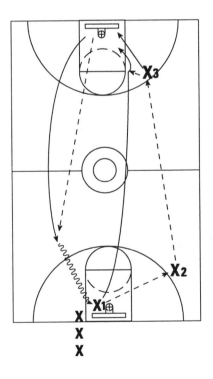

Drill #77: Non-Stop Lay-Up Drill

Objective: To develop lay-up and passing skills; to enhance conditioning levels.

Description: The drill begins with six players positioned as passers, and the rest of the team divided into two lines of shooters. Each shooter should have a basketball. The drill begins with the first shooter in each line passing to the first passer on his side of the court and sprinting upcourt. X1 hits X2, who hits X3. X3 passes to the sprinting shooter, who drives for the lay-up. After a set amount of time, the passers and shooters switch roles.

Coaching Point:

- The coach should vary the duration of the drill according the desired level of conditioning.

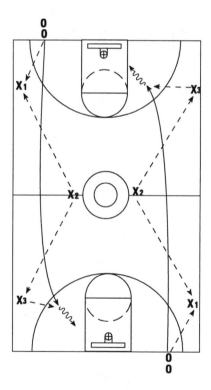

Drill #78: Four-Player Weave Lay-Up Drill

Objective: To develop ball-handling and lay-up shooting skills in a warm-up situation.

Description: The coach should divide the squad into groups of four players, who are positioned as shown in the diagram below. X1 begins the drill by passing to the wing on his side (X2), who returns the pass and begins the weave. X1 hands off on the outside, and the weave continues with the players always going to the inside when handing off and to the outside when receiving the ball. On the coach's whistle, the player with the ball breaks off and drives to the basket for a lay-up with the other three players following to rebound.

Coaching Point:

- This drill is an excellent warm-up drill since the pace can be varied from leisurely to full speed.

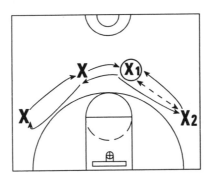

Drill #79: Lay-Up Passing Competition Drill

Objective: To develop passing and lay-up skills in a full-speed competitive situation; to enhance conditioning levels.

Description: The coach should divide the team into groups of four players, positioned as shown in the diagram below. X1 begins the drill by making a lay-up, rebounding, and passing to X2. X1 sprints upcourt while X2 passes to X3. X3 passes to X4, who hits X1 in full stride for the lay-up. X1 again rebounds his own shot and speed dribbles the length of the floor and takes a third lay-up. The lay-ups must be made for the players to rotate positions. The first team to have all four players finish wins.

Coaching Points:

- The coach may wish to have all players shoot and dribble with their off hand.
- For additional conditioning and to increase the competitive atmosphere, the coach can make losers either run additional line sprints or perform calisthenics.

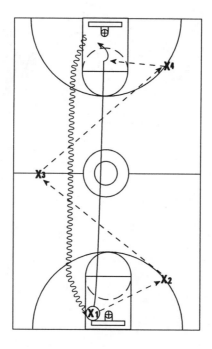

Drill #80: Lay-Up Jump-Shot Speed Drill

Objective: To teach players to shoot lay-ups and jump-shots at full speed; to develop stamina.

Description: The drill involves three players and two basketballs at a time. A coach or manager should be designated as a timekeeper. Players X1 and X2 are instructed to rebound each shot and return each ball to its original position at each end of the foul line. X3 faces the basket in the middle of the lane, and, on the timekeeper's command, runs to the ball on his right and takes it to the hoop for a right-handed lay-up. He then races to the second ball and takes a jump-shot from the left side of the foul line. X3 repeats this process for a set period of time. X1 and X2 then rotate into the shooter's position. When X3 begins the second rotation, he reverses the process by driving for left-handed lay-ups and shooting jump-shots from the right side of the foul line.

Coaching Point:

- The coach should set the time allowed for each player to complete a rotation according to the ability and conditioning level of his players. Each player usually operates in the shooter's position for a period of 30 to 60 seconds. Each three-player group should complete the drill within six minutes.

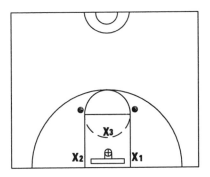

Drill #81: Contested Lay-Up Drill

Objective: To teach players to protect the ball while going strong to the hoop for a contested lay-up.

Description: The coach should divide the squad into equal lines with one at the top of the key on offense and the other at the sideline on defense. The first offensive player drives hard to the hoop, while the defender comes hard to block the lay-up. The players then go to the end of the opposite line.

Coaching Points:

- Coaches should stop the drill to be sure offensive players are protecting the ball and concentrating on the spot.
- Defenders should be taught to attempt a block with their inside hand.

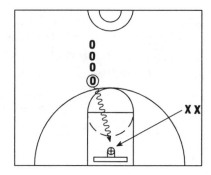

CHAPTER 8

POST PLAY DRILLS

Drill #82: Feed the Post Drill

Objective: To teach the basic moves involved in getting open to receive a pass into the post.

Description: The entire team rotates into this drill in groups of two—one player on offense and the other on defense. The coach or a designated point guard acts as the passer on the wing. The offensive post player begins various moves from the far side of the lane, working to get open while the defender tries to deny the pass. Facing moves resulting in a jump-shot, crossover post moves utilizing a front turn, and power and spin moves should all be used. The drill should continue until all players have rotated into both offensive and defensive positions on both sides of the lane.

Coaching Points:

- The coach may wish to designate which post move the player should use to make sure all the basic moves are practiced.
- Body position, footwork, and proper pass reception techniques should be emphasized.

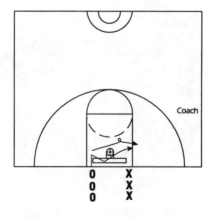

Drill #83: Power Move Post Drill

Objective: To teach post players fundamentals of power post maneuvers.

Description: This drill is designed for the post players only. Each player should practice pivoting on his non-baseline foot and using his dominant hand for a shot off the backboard. Next, he should add a dribble to the basic move, concentrating on maintaining his balance and using the dribble to move him into position to take the shot. Another variation the player should practice is adding a head fake when picking up his dribble. In this move, the player should work on keeping the ball at shoulder level before going up for the shot.

Coaching Point:

- The coach should observe each player closely and make sure the proper techniques, not bad habits, are being practiced.

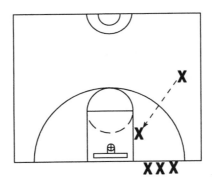

Drill #84: Turn and Face Drill

Objective: To teach post players fundamentals of turn and face maneuvers.

Description: This drill is designed for post players, but requires a player or coach to act as a defender. The post player practices variations of turning and facing the basket. With the defender behind him, the post player turns to face the basket, squares up, and then makes a move to the hoop. He should then practice turning to face the middle and using a dribble move. A third variation involves turning to face the baseline and dribbling back to the middle for a hook shot. Finally, the player should work on turning to face the basket and adding a lift fake to the power dribble move. The defender should offer token resistance or aggressive pressure as determined by the coach.

Coaching Point:

- The coach should observe each player closely and make sure the proper techniques, not bad habits, are being practiced.

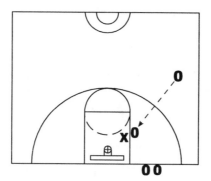

Drill #85: One-on-One Post Game

Objective: To develop one-on-one skills with the help of a post player.

Description: Three players are positioned as shown in the diagram below. The ball is in the post player's hands (C), and X1 and X2 have their backs to the basket. On the coach's whistle, C rolls the ball toward midcourt, and X1 and X2 scramble to gain possession. Whoever gets to the ball first is on offense, and the two engage in one-on-one half-court basketball. Points are awarded as follows: +2 for a field goal; +1 for a defensive foul; -1 for an offensive foul; +1 for a pass into the post; -1 for a turnover; and +1 for an offensive rebound. The coach calls out the points to the manager, who acts as scorekeeper. The ball changes possession on defensive rebounds and turnovers. The offensive player may pass into the post and move without the ball to get open for a return pass, or use the post player for a screen. The post player may move to the high or low post as ball position dictates, but may not shoot, rebound, or dribble. The game continues for a set period of time, and the player with the highest point total is declared the winner.

Coaching Point:

- The coach should emphasize protecting the ball, movement without the ball, good passes, and proper use of the screen.

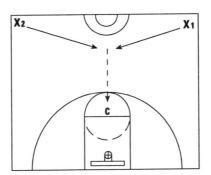

Drill #86: Three-on-Three Post Game

Objective: To develop skills in passing to the post and splitting the post in a competitive atmosphere.

Description: The coach divides the squad into six-player teams, three players on offense and three on defense. The players may use the entire half court and may earn points in various ways. Each offensive team has the ball for a designated amount of time and then switches with the defense. The team that scores the most points wins the game. Points are awarded as follows: +1 when the pass goes to a post player and is followed by a split-the-post maneuver; -1 for an offensive foul; +1 for a defensive foul; +2 for a made field goal; and +1 for an offensive rebound. The coach calls out the points to the manager, who acts as scorekeeper. No free throws are taken, and the ball always goes back to the offense.

Coaching Point:

- The coach should make sure the passer always goes first when executing the split-the-post maneuver.

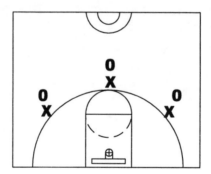

Drill #87: Four-on-One Post Drill

Objective: To improve skills in getting open to receive a pass in the post; to work on various moves to the basket once a pass has been received.

Description: This drill should be run at full speed. Four offensive players and one defensive player are positioned as shown in the diagram below. The perimeter players pass the ball among themselves as the post player works to get open and the defender tries to deny the pass. Post players may work between the high post and low post, but may not go out past the free-throw line. After receiving the pass, the post player practices various moves to the basket. The coach may also choose to run this drill with no defense or token defense. Defenders can also be placed on the perimeter to make the pass more difficult.

Coaching Points:

- Correct body positioning on both offense and defense should be emphasized.
- The coach should encourage the post player to work on a variety of moves.

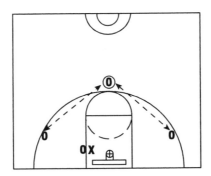

Drill #88: Seven-on-Two Post Drill

Objective: To develop post players' skills in getting open to receive a pass.

Description: Seven offensive and two defensive players are positioned as shown in the diagram below, with the ball in a point guard's hands. The outside players pass the ball around the perimeter, looking for an opportunity to pass the ball into the post. The two post players use a variety of moves to attempt to get open to receive the pass and the defenders try to deny the ball. Post players can break from the low to high post, but can not go out past the free-throw line. The coach may also run the drill either with no defense or against token defense.

Coaching Points:

- The coach should encourage post players to use screens, spin and reverse spin moves, and positioning for a lob pass to get the ball.
- Correct body positioning on both offense and defense should be emphasized.

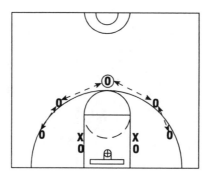

CHAPTER 9

OFFENSIVE REBOUND DRILLS

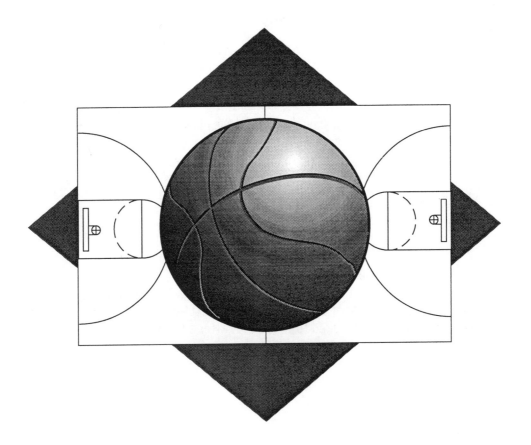

Drill #89: Ante-Over

Objective: To practice rebounding techniques, footwork, tipping, and ball control.

Description: The drill involves groups of three players at a basket. The middle player has a ball and starts the drill with a pass off the backboard (above the rectangle, which is over the rim) to the opposite player. The player receiving the pass tips the pass off the backboard to the player on the other side and then goes behind the player to whom the ball is tipped. The passer (initially the original middle player) assumes the position of the player who tipped the ball. The basic goal of the drill is to achieve continuous, controlled tipping by the group for a given number of repetitions.

Coaching points:

- Players should keep their hands above their shoulders all of the time the ball is in play.
- Players should jump off of both feet and use two hands to capture the ball.
- Players should keep their elbows extended and use their fingers and wrists.
- Players should keep the ball above the rectangle and control the tip (catch and shoot the ball).
- The player tipping the ball should go behind the player to whom the ball is tipped.
- Each player should move quickly to the next spot; players should not slide and stare at the ball. Groups should be composed of players of equal size and jumping ability.

Variations:

- Players should first use either hand to tip.
- After players do well, they should be required to tip with their right hand when they're on the right side of the basket and their left hand when on the left side.
- Every player could be required to shoot a 1+1 after each rebound.

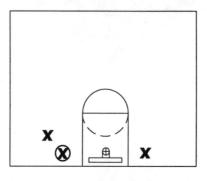

Drill #90: Two-Player Box-Out Switch

Objective: To practice clearing-out techniques and to develop footwork.

Description: The drill involves four players—two on defense (X) and two on offense (O). The two (O)s stand behind the foul line, slightly outside the foul lane area. The two (X)s assume a position outside the foul lane area, approximately six feet closer to the basket than the (O)s. The drill begins by having the coach (C) take a shot. As soon as the shot is released, the (O)s attempt to crash the boards to get an offensive rebound. The (X)s clear out the opposite (O)s. The (X)s then crash the boards to get the rebound. If the (X)s get the rebound, the players switch roles. If the (O)s get the rebound, the drill is repeated with the players in the same roles.

Coaching point:

- The coach should ensure that proper techniques and footwork are used and make corrections as necessary.

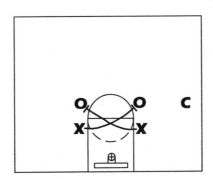

Drill #91: Two-Line Rebounding

Objective: To teach boxing out and the techniques of aggressive rebounding; to develop the ability to make outlet passes; to improve offensive rebounding skills.

Description: The players form two lines facing the basket, one at each end of the free throw line. The first player in each line acts as a defensive player (X), while all of the other players serve offensive (O) roles. The drill begins by having the coach (C) shoot the ball. The two (X)s then box out the first player in each line (O). The two (O)s crash the board, while the (X)s attempt to hold them out, rebound the missed shot, and throw an outlet pass to a manager (M) positioned in the outlet area. The two (O)s then go to the end of the line and are replaced by the next man in each line. The drill continues with the same (X)s against all of the (O)s—two at a time. Once the (X)s have defended against all of the (O)s, they go to the end of the offensive player line and two new defenders take their place.

Coaching Points:

- The coach should move the lines to practice rebounding from different areas and positions.
- A reasonable amount of physical contact should be permitted.
- A scoring system should be used that rewards the defenders who get the most rebounds.
- The (C) and (M) should have a choice of a variety of options: (1) shoot immediately; (2) pass to each other and then shoot; or (3) pass to one of the (O)s who then shoots.

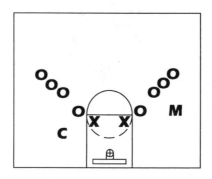

Drill #92: Three-Man Bound and Break

Objective: To practice rebounding techniques, outlet passing, footwork, and fast break movement patterns.

Description: The drill involves three rebounders and two wing players. The drill begins by having the coach shoot from the free throw line. P-1, P-2, and P-3 aggressively go for the rebound. Whoever gets the rebound outlets a pass to the open wing player (enter P-4 or P-6). While waiting for the outlet pass, P-4 and P-6 execute multiple moves to get open. P-5 and P-7 defend against the outlet pass. Upon retrieving the ball, the rebounder has three primary options:

- Pass to the open wing on the rebounder's side of the court.
- Pass to the opposite wing, who is cutting to the middle of the court.
- Dribble the ball out and then pass to an open wing.

After making an outlet pass, the rebounder goes on a fast break with the two wing players (P-4 and P-6). Together they work to get the ball out of the backcourt. All other players wait to rotate into the drill.

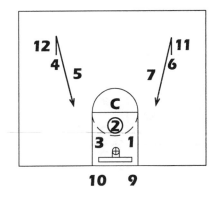

Drill # 93: Two-Ball Rebounding

Objective: To teach rebounders to make a continuous effort to go for the ball; to practice both clearing-out and rebounding techniques.

Description: The drill involves three-on-three competition between offensive players (O) and defensive players (X). The drill begins by having the coach (C) shoot a ball. As soon as the (X)s control the rebound of that shot, the manager (M) shoots a second ball. Both the (X)s and the (O)s aggressively attempt to rebound both shots. The (X)s outlet each rebound they retrieve to the (C) or (M). Offensive rebounds are put back up by the (O)s. Once a shot is made by the (O)s, the drill stops.

Coaching point:

- The coach should ensure that proper techniques and footwork are used and make corrections as necessary.
- All players should be encouraged to aggressively pursue each rebound.

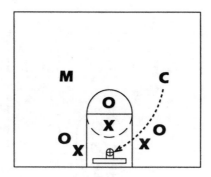

Drill # 94: Aggressive Rebounding

Objective: To increase aggressiveness while rebounding and to develop the ability to withstand the contact and pressure which occurs during rebounding.

Description: The players form three lines. The first player in each line competes against the first player in the other two lines. The three competing players assume a position in front of and facing the basket. The drill begins by having the coach (C) toss the ball off the backboard. All three players compete for the rebound. The player getting the rebound becomes the offensive player and attempts to score against the other two players who then go on defense. Once a score is made, the drill is repeated with the same three players until one player scores two baskets. If an offensive player misses the shot and the ball stays in the lane, the player getting the rebound then goes on offense against the other two players. Once a player scores twice, that player goes to the end of that player's line. The first group of players in a line to get all of the players through is the winner. On a made shot or a ball that rebounds outside the lane area, the ball goes back to the (C) and the drill is repeated.

Coaching Points:

- Players should be encouraged to play with intensity and aggressiveness.
- Physical contact should be ignored.
- All shots should be put back up aggressively—not with finesse.
- Players should keep their hands up.

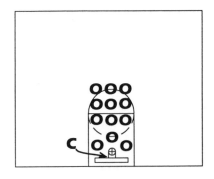

Drill 95: Over-and-Back Tapping

Objective: To develop stamina, to practice timing and quick jumping.

Description: The drill involves two players at a time. The two players line up facing the basket on opposite sides of the foul lane. The drill commences by having one player tap the ball over the basket to the other player. They then continue to tap the ball back and forth to each other for a preset number of times or a predetermined period of time. If they allow the ball to hit the floor, the drill (and the count) begins again.

Coaching points:

- The coach can require the players to alternate the hand used to tip the ball.
- The proper techniques for tipping must be followed.

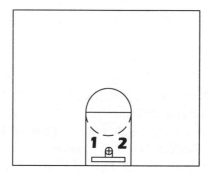

CHAPTER 10

OUT-OF-BOUNDS DRILLS

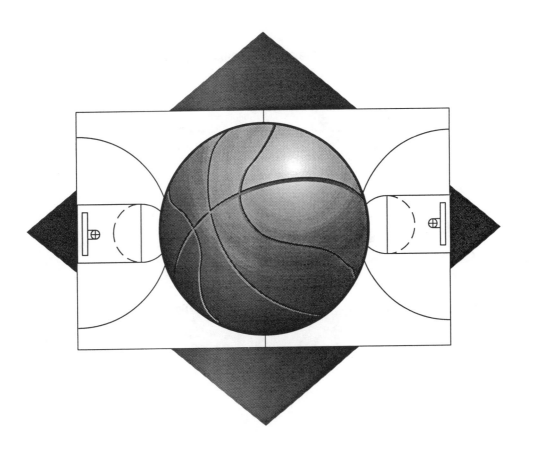

Drill #96: Double Up

Objective: To safely inbound the ball; to create scoring opportunities against a man-to-man defense.

Description: The drill begins with the ball in the small forward's (SF) hands and the offense positioned as shown in Diagram A. Both post players move up the lane to set screens for the shooting guard (SG) and the point guard (PG). SG breaks off the screen by the center (C) and receives the inbound pass. Then, as shown in Diagram B, SF moves up the lane to set a screen for the power forward (PF), who breaks off the screen to the low post. C then slides across the lane and sets a screen for SF. SF cuts off the screen to the ballside for a pass to take the short jumper. This play is designed to create three options for SG. He may take the quick jumper after receiving the inbound pass, or look to PF down low or SF outside.

Coaching Point:

*   This play is especially effective against teams who like to play close man-to-man defense.

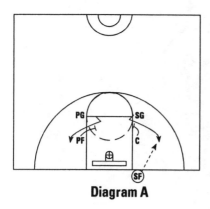

Diagram A

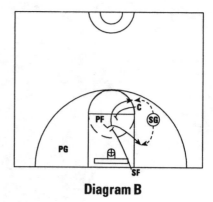

Diagram B

Drill #97: Around the Horn to the Backdoor

Objective: To safely inbound the ball using a stack set.

Description: The drill begins with the ball in the point guard's (PG) hands and the rest of the offense positioned as shown in Diagram A. The small forward (SF) moves down the lane to screen for the center (C). C breaks off the pick to the outside wing. The power forward (PF) crosses the lane diagonally to the ballside wing. This clears the offside of the floor. The shooting guard (SG) breaks out to take the inbound pass, and PG moves to the offside low wing. SG starts the ball around the horn to PF, who passes to C. Meanwhile, PG has been attempting to get his defender to overplay to open up the backdoor opportunity. If the defender is too aggressive, the backdoor should be there. If the defender is playing soft, C passes down to PG on the wing (Diagram B). The SF sets a screen for PF, who breaks down the lane. SF cuts off a pick from C to the top of the key. PG either finds PF in the lane or goes to SF for the jump-shot.

Coaching Points:

- The importance of breaking hard to the wing after the inbound pass to attempt to get the chasing defender out of control should be emphasized to PG.

- Rapid ball movement around the perimeter should also be stressed.

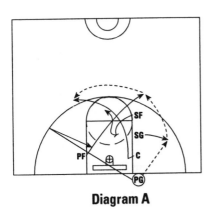

Diagram A

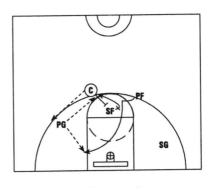

Diagram B

Objective: To safely inbound the ball using a diamond set.

Description: This drill begins with the players positioned as illustrated in Diagram A. The small forward (SF) cuts to the corner to clear out the low post. The center (C) moves quickly across the lane looking for the inbound pass. The power forward (PF) fakes as if to join the action on the ball side and V-cuts to the low post position vacated by C. The shooting guard's (SG) first option is to look to the big players down low. Meanwhile, the point guard (PG) moves outside and becomes SG's second choice for the inbound pass. As the pass is made, C posts up in the lane looking for the pass from PG, and SG moves to the offside wing behind a pick from PF (Diagram B). PG may hit SG coming off the screen, or find C, who can either turn for the jumper or deliver the ball to SG. The third choice is shown in Diagram C. SG passes to SF in the corner. As the pass is made, C moves across the lane and sets a pick for the inbounder. SG loops around the screen looking for the return pass from SF and slips into the lane for a jumper.

Coaching Point:

- The inbounder should look specifically to the three options in the order listed above.

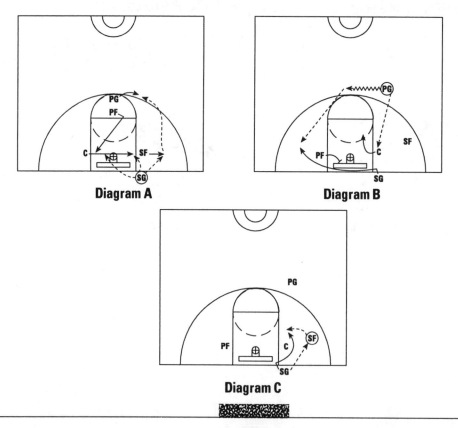

Diagram A   Diagram B

Diagram C

Drill #99: PG's Choice

Objective: To safely inbound the ball using a random set.

Description: The drill begins with the players positioned as illustrated in the diagram below. The point guard (PG) gets into position to receive a pass from the shooting guard (SG), who has cut to the corner to take the inbound pass. The small forward (SF) streaks toward the power forward (PF) on the far side of the lane. If SF's defender gets out of control trying to keep up, SF stops short and stays low behind the center (C) for a pass from PG and the easy jumper. If not, SF continues on and stacks up with PF at the edge of the lane. SG clears to the opposite wing around a screen set by C, PF, and SF. PG now has two more options available. He can dribble toward SG and pass to either SG or SF, who has broken off his screen and up the lane toward the ball. PG can also dribble back to the spot vacated by SG. From there, PG can pass into C on the post and start a two-player game.

Coaching Point:

- This drill offers a particularly appropriate option if PG is a sound player physically and mentally.

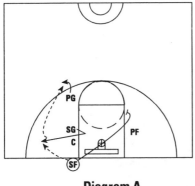

Diagram A

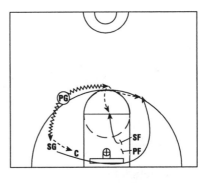

Diagram B

Drill #100: Five In a Line

Objective: To safely inbound the ball in a side-out situation; to practice a play designed to produce a three-point shot.

Description: The drill begins with the shooting guard (SG) inbounding the ball and the rest of the offense in a straight line near half-court as illustrated in Diagram A. The point guard (PG) breaks from the end of the line and cuts around the stack toward the baseline. He should be ahead of his defender. If PG is open, SG gives up the ball immediately, and PG moves down for the quick three-point attempt. If PG does not get the ball, SF breaks out of the line and takes the inbound pass. The next attempt to get a three-point shot is shown in Diagram B. The power forward (PF) and center (C) step down and set a double screen. After inbounding, SG drives toward the lane to set up his defender. He then reverse cuts around the barricade to receive a pass from SF, and attempts a three-point shot if he is open. If SG cannot get the pass, C and PF move down to set a screen for PG. PG cuts off the screen back to the top of the key looking for a pass from SF to take the three-pointer.

Coaching Point:

- The best chance for an open shot is the first option. A coach should adjust his personnel so his best three-point shooter is coming off the back of the stack.

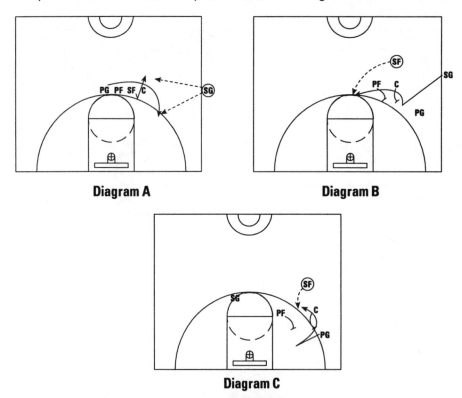

Diagram A   Diagram B

Diagram C

Drill #101: Isolate C

Objective: To safely inbound the ball in a side-out situation; to isolate the center in the post.

Description: This drill begins with the small forward (SF) inbounding the ball near half-court and the other players positioned as illustrated in the diagram below. The center (C) moves into the center of the lane to set a pick for the point guard (PG). PG starts toward the screen as if he is going to use it, then breaks sharply up the lane line instead. The power forward (PF) moves across the lane to the elbow to set a pick for the shooting guard (SG). SG cuts off the pick toward the inbounder to take the pass from SF. PF remains in position and sets a second pick for PG as he comes up the lane to take position at the offside top of the key. After inbounding, SF stays high to act as a safety with PG. SG dribbles toward the ballside wing and passes into C, who is alone in the lane. The one-on-one post game then commences.

Coaching Point:

- If C's defender overplays between the ball and C, C seals the defender, creating the opportunity for a lob pass.

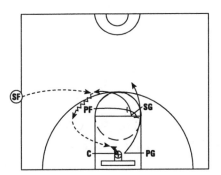

George Karl is the head coach of the Seattle SuperSonics. Since assuming his present position on January 23, 1992, Karl has led the Sonics to over 300 victories. A 1973 graduate of North Carolina where he played three years for Dean Smith's Tar Heels and gained All-American honors as a senior, Karl began his distinguished coaching career in 1978 as an assistant in the ABA for the San Antonio Spurs. After two seasons with the Spurs, Karl then moved to the Continental Basketball Association as the head coach of the Montana Golden Nuggets. After three years with the Golden Nuggets, he began his NBA head coaching career with the Cleveland Cavaliers in 1984. Two years later, Karl accepted the same position with the Golden State Warriors—a job he held for two seasons. Subsequently, Karl spent two additional seasons each with the CBA's

Jeff Reinking Photography

Terry Stotts, George Karl, Price Johnson (L-R)

Albany Patroons and with Real Madrid of the Spanish League. One of the most respected and knowledgeable coaches in the game, Karl resides in the Seattle area with his wife Cathy and their two children—Kelci and Coby.

Terry Stotts is an assistant coach with the Seattle SuperSonics. He began his career with the Sonics in 1992 as a scout, before assuming his present position prior to the start of the 1993-94 season. A 1980 graduate of the University of Oklahoma where he earned numerous honors as a basketball player for the Sooners, Stotts began his coaching career in 1990 as an assistant coach with the Albany Patroons under current Sonic head coach George Karl. He then spent one season as an assistant with the CBA's Fort Wayne Fury, before joining the Sonics staff. Terry and his wife Jan reside in the Seattle area.

Price Johnson is a successful youth basketball coach and basketball camp director in the Bellevue, Washington area. For the past 15 years, he has worked both as coach and as advocate of youth basketball. Since 1992, Johnson has taken an all-star youth basketball team to the national tournament for youth basketball, placing in the top 10 teams each year. Johnson is a co-owner of Hoopaholics, a successful sportswear company. Price and his wife of 16 years, Julianne, reside in Bellevue, Washington with their two sons—James and Dane.